William Power Burnham

Three Roads to a Commission in the United States Army

William Power Burnham

Three Roads to a Commission in the United States Army

ISBN/EAN: 9783744728270

Printed in Europe, USA, Canada, Australia, Japan

Cover: Foto ©Suzi / pixelio.de

More available books at **www.hansebooks.com**

THREE ROADS
TO A COMMISSION IN THE
UNITED STATES ARMY

BY

LIEUT. W. P. BURNHAM
SIXTH U. S. INFANTRY
AUTHOR OF
MANUAL OF OUTPOST DUTY, ADVANCE AND REAR GUARDS,
MILITARY TRAINING OF THE UNITED STATES ARMY, ETC.

NEW YORK
D. APPLETON AND COMPANY
1899

COPYRIGHT, 1893,
BY D. APPLETON AND COMPANY.

ELECTROTYPED AND PRINTED
AT THE APPLETON PRESS, U. S. A.

PREFACE.

THE idea of preparing this handbook suggested itself to me shortly after assuming the duties of Professor of Military Science and Tactics at St. John's Military School, Manlius, New York.

I was surprised to find so much interest manifested in the army, and yet more surprised to find how little was known of its real workings. The most remarkable impressions were entertained regarding the character, hardships, and privations of the rank and file of the army. However, this was not new, for experience had proved to me that, as a rule, the average American believes the army is the receptacle of drunkards and loafers, and that the riffraff of the country is to be found in its ranks. Little seemed to be known as to the manner of entering the Military Academy, the nature of the preliminary examinations, and the course pursued after entrance. The fact that a commission could easily be obtained from the ranks of the army was beyond comprehension, many not knowing that such a thing was possible in time of peace.

Believing that similar ignorance on this subject was general throughout the country, I decided, during my spare moments, to endeavor to lift the veil that obscures and darkens the view of the best fed, best clothed, best paid, and best standing army in the world.

During the years 1891 and 1892 the character and extent of the examinations for obtaining a commission from the ranks of the army and from civil life were considerably changed. While the *extent* and *character* of the preliminary examination for entrance to the National Academy are the same as heretofore, the *place* and *manner* of conducting it were changed materially in 1892.

The rules governing the various examinations are taken from the official records of the War Department, which are based on acts of Congress; and these regulations are so stated that the reader will easily distinguish what is regularly prescribed from such original remarks and explanations as it has been considered pertinent to make.

I am indebted to Lieut. J. M. Carson, Jr., Fifth Cavalry, adjutant of the Military Academy, for the very latest information regarding the requirements for entrance and the course of study pursued at that institution. I am grateful also to a number of other officers who kindly assisted me in obtaining the valuable lists of questions propounded at the different examinations.

W. P. BURNHAM,
First Lieutenant, Sixth Infantry.

ST. JOHN'S MILITARY SCHOOL,
    MANLIUS, N. Y., *December 5, 1892.*

CONTENTS.

CHAPTER I.

	PAGE
Extract from Army Regulations	1
Commissions from the United States Military Academy.	2
Method of appointment	6
Manner of making applications	7
Hints to aspiring candidates	10
Expenses prior to entrance	15
Character of entrance examinations	15
Points in regard to entrance examination	27
When and where examinations are held	29
The new cadet	31
Pay of cadets	34
Length of service in the army	36
Academic duties	37
Assignments after graduation	44
Questions asked at entrance examination	47

CHAPTER II.

Commissions from the ranks of the army	58
The preliminary examination	61
The final examination	65

CONTENTS.

	PAGE
Method of making application	70
Method of selection	71
Character of examinations	72
Hints to competitors	73
Assignment to regiment	75
Enlisting for a commission	76
Selection of arm of service	81
Pay and discharges	82
Examination questions, final board	83

CHAPTER III.

Commissions from civil life	109
Character of examinations	110
Manner of making application	115
Place and method of examination	116
Hints to candidates	117
Assignment to regiment	121
Examination questions	123

APPENDIX.

Course of study at the Military Academy	141
Form of appointment to the Military Academy	148
Articles of agreement and oath of cadet at the Military Academy	150
Oath and form of enlistment papers of recruit in the regular army	151
Form for physical examination of recruit in the regular army	154
List and location of recruiting offices of the regular army	156
Oath of office for an officer of the regular army	158
Table of pay allowed by law to officers	160

THREE ROADS TO A COMMISSION
IN THE UNITED STATES ARMY.

CHAPTER I.

FROM THE UNITED STATES MILITARY ACADEMY.

EXTRACT FROM ARMY REGULATIONS.

THE three roads to a commission in the line of the United States Regular Army are briefly outlined in paragraph 23, Army Regulations, 1889, which is as follows:

"Vacancies in the grade of second lieutenant are filled by appointment from the graduates of the Military Academy, so long as any such remain in service unassigned. Vacancies thereafter are filled by appointment of meritorious soldiers favorably recommended in accordance with act of Congress approved June 30, 1892.

"Vacancies existing after exhausting the two classes named may be filled by appointment from civil life. Appointments of civilians, except of graduates of the Military Academy who have been honorably discharged, will not be made in time of peace unless more vacancies exist than will be required in the assignment of the next graduating class."

Appointments to the medical department and other staff corps are not considered in this volume.

COMMISSIONS FROM THE UNITED STATES MILITARY ACADEMY.

The National Academy is located at West Point, N. Y., on the right bank of the Hudson River, about fifty miles from New York city. The academy is situated on a plain about one hundred and seventy feet above the river, and is surrounded by the bold and romantic scenery of one of the finest river passes in the world. The academy can be reached by rail or boat from New York city or Albany.

West Point was occupied as a military station during the Revolutionary War, being captured by the British in 1777, but abandoned after Burgoyne's surrender, when more formidable forts were constructed. It was these the traitor General Arnold attempted to betray, the plot having been foiled by the arrest of Major André, the circumstances of which are well known by the average American schoolboy.

The academy was established in 1802, being designed originally for an engineer school, and capable of instructing fifty cadets.

In 1843 the present method of appointment was adopted, since which time its capacity has been increased to meet the corresponding growth of the republic, until now it is capable of instructing about four hundred cadets, and from this source come the majority of the commissioned officers of the regular standing army of the United States.

The school is governed and instructed by a superintendent and an academic board consisting of seven professors assisted by about sixty instructors and assistant instructors. The professors remain permanently at the academy, being appointed to their positions by the War Department. The superintendent and the instructors belong to the different branches of the army, being selected on account of their special fitness for the duty; but the period of their detail is limited usually to four years, when they are relieved by other suitable officers. The academy is inspected annually by an inspector-general of the army, and also by a board of visitors, which is composed of twelve members; seven of them are appointed by the President of the United States; the remainder of the board consists of three members of the House of Representatives, appointed by the Speaker, and two Senators, designated by the President of the Senate. The board makes a careful examination into the workings of the institution and reports the result of its investigations to the President, with such recommendations as it may deem expedient.

The course of study is shown in a tabulated form in the Appendix, from which can be gathered an approximate idea of the amount of theoretical and practical instruction imparted during the course of four years.

The cadets are arranged in four classes, corresponding with the four years of study. The fourth class is employed on the first year's course, and hence corresponds to the "freshman" class at most colleges; the third class corresponds to the "sophomore" class, being engaged in the second year's work; the second class, corresponding to the "junior" class, is at work on the third year's course; and, finally, the first class, pursuing the last year's duties, corresponds to the "senior" class at most institutions.

Each class is divided into sections consisting of from eight to twelve cadets, and from time to time cadets are sent from a higher to a lower section, or the reverse, depending upon their aptitude and proficiency.

A weekly statement is posted on the bulletin board showing each cadet's relative progress in his studies. In addition to this the superintendent sends a monthly statement to the parent of each cadet, which exhibits his standing both as to his studies and conduct.

As each of these sections has an instructor, and as the recitations are from an hour to an hour and a half in length, a cadet's knowledge of each lesson is thoroughly tested.

For purposes of discipline and military instruction the corps of cadets is divided into four companies, each consisting of about seventy-five cadets. The companies are composed of about an equal number of cadets from each class. Each company is under the general management of an experienced army officer, known as a "tactical" officer, the entire corps or battalion being governed by an officer with the rank of lieutenant-colonel, known as the commandant. In addition to this each company is officered by a cadet captain, two or three cadet lieutenants, and ten or twelve cadet non-commissioned officers. Usually the cadet officers are selected from the first class, the cadet sergeants from the second class, and the cadet corporals from the third class.

The military routine and discipline at West Point are followed closely by a few of the civilian preparatory schools of the United States, as it has been demonstrated that the routine and military training at the National Academy produce the best of results, especially in preparing boys for college.

METHOD OF MAKING APPOINTMENTS.

Each congressional district and Territory, also the District of Columbia, is entitled to have one cadet at the academy. The appointments are made by the Secretary of War at the request of the Representative or Delegate in Congress from the district or Territory; and the person appointed must be an actual resident of the district or Territory from which the appointment is made.

Ten are also appointed by the President, being known as appointments *at large*, and are especially conferred by the President of the United States.

"The Representative or Delegate in Congress may nominate a legally qualified second candidate, to be designated the *alternate*.

"The alternate will receive from the War Department a letter of appointment, and will be examined *with the regular appointee*, and, if duly qualified, will be admitted to the academy in the event of the failure of the principal to pass the prescribed preliminary examination. The alternate will not be allowed to defer reporting for examination until the result of the examination of the regular appointee is known, but must report at the time and place designated in his letter of appointment. The alternate, like the nominee, should be designated as nearly one year in advance of date of admission as possible."

Manner of Making Application.

Application may be made at any time by letter to the Secretary of War to have the name of the applicant placed upon the file, that it may be furnished to the proper Representative or Delegate when a vacancy occurs. The application should give the full name, age, and residence of the applicant, with the number of the congressional district in which his home is located. As a rule, appointments are required to be made one year in advance of the date of admission. The age of admission for cadets to the academy is between seventeen and twenty-two years. A candidate desiring appointment to the academy, and having had his name placed on the register at the War Department, will not necessarily receive the desired appointment, further effort usually being required. As soon as it is learned that there is to be a vacancy at the academy from his district the applicant should apply to the Congressman for appointment to it, forwarding such recommendations as to fitness for the position as he can obtain, giving full particulars as to age, residence, health, education, etc., and requesting in respectful terms that his name may receive consideration in filling the vacancy.

A vacancy from a district may result from various causes. Some of these are the graduation of the cadet representing it, his discharge, dismissal, or resignation from the academy. At all events, it would be well for the candidate to apply to his Congressman at least a year before the probable graduation of the cadet he desires to succeed. It is becoming quite common for competitive examinations to be held in a district when a vacancy at West Point from that district occurs. In this case the Representative will inform such applicants as he desires to compete to appear for examination at a certain time and place, usually stating the scope of the examination. The applicant who passes the most satisfactory examination is selected and his name sent to the Secretary of War, with the request that an appointment be issued. The applicant who passes the next best examination may be appointed as alternate. It must be borne in mind, however, that the selection of an applicant for appointment to West Point rests entirely with the Representative of the district, and he is at liberty to make it in any manner he sees fit. He may select one of his friends, one of his enemies, or he may elect to have a competitive examination with a view to getting the best boy for the place, or from any other motive.

The ten appointments *at large* which are made by the President of the United States were designed originally for the benefit of the sons of army officers who, having no permanent abode, are thus debarred from getting an appointment in the usual way. As just explained, however, it rests solely with the President as to the persons appointed and the manner of selecting the applicant. Applications for appointments *at large* are made to the Secretary of War (sometimes to the President himself), and should contain all that is necessary for the President to determine the fitness of the applicant. Great influence is brought to bear in the interests of applicants for this class of appointments, but as a rule the sons of meritorious army officers have received a share of them.

The Secretary of War will furnish the successful applicant with an appointment (see blank form in Appendix), and direct him to report in person to the president of a certain board of officers on a certain day, to be examined for entrance to the United States Military Academy.

No person who is married will be admitted to the academy as a cadet; and should a cadet marry after entrance, it will be equivalent to a resignation, and he will be required to leave the academy at once.

Hints to Aspiring Candidates.

Before accepting an appointment to the Military Academy a young man should satisfy himself that he is mentally and physically qualified to undergo the discipline and pursue his course at the academy to a successful termination.

To this end, first of all note the fact that the physical examination is extremely rigid; and if you have any suspicion that you are not physically sound, a reliable surgeon or physician should be consulted. Tell him exactly what is required, and ask him to make a careful examination, as is laid down for the preliminary examination for entrance. If he finds any defects which would render you unfit for military service, further effort on your part to enter the academy may as well be abandoned, thus saving you and the Government considerable time and money. The eyes should receive special attention, as many young men have defective eyes who suppose that they are perfectly sound. Color blindness, far- and near-sightedness, are much more common than is generally known.

"A sound body and constitution, suitable preparation, good natural capacity, an aptitude for study, industrious habits, perseverance, an obedient and orderly disposition, and correct moral deportment, are such essential qualifications that candidates knowingly deficient in any of these respects should not, as many do, subject themselves and their friends to the chances of future mortification and disappointment by accepting appointments at the academy and entering upon a course which they can not successfully pursue."

This is good, wholesome advice from the Secretary of War to aspirants for military glory at West Point.

Going somewhat into the details of this very important subject, it must be remembered that by suitable preparation is meant not only that *you are properly prepared to pass the entrance examination*, but it means that you should be partially prepared on a portion of the course pursued *after entering*. You will see, by referring to the course of study (see Appendix), that during the first year the course in mathematics goes through algebra, geometry, trigonometry, surveying, and a portion of analytical geometry.

Besides this, a portion of the French and English courses is studied. You will admit that there is not another institution in this country that attempts to give thorough instruction in algebra, geometry, trigonometry, and surveying in a single year. It seems to be assumed at West Point that cadets have a fair knowledge of many of these subjects, and hence they are gone over very rapidly, similar to a "general review," but the most thorough knowledge is exacted of the cadet. There can be no shirking, for if the why and wherefore of each point is not known you will suffer accordingly. Hence it would be well for you not to enter the academy until you have more or less mastered a portion of the course of study pursued the first year after entrance. Also, note the words, "good natural capacity" and "industrious habits." Many go to

West Point and pass excellent entrance examinations, and yet are discharged for deficiency in studies in less than a year. In some cases this is due to what is vulgarly known as "cramming" for the entrance examination, and neglecting to be prepared on subjects of higher mathematics. In other cases it is due to careful preparation for entrance, and lack of natural capacity to grasp the meaning of more advanced studies.

It is safe to predict that a boy with only an average capacity for mathematics, and who, upon entering the academy, has never studied algebra, will be found deficient in mathematics inside of six months. Again, it is equally safe to predict that if you have an average capacity for mathematics, and have a fair knowledge of algebra, geometry, and trigonometry upon entering, and are possessed of "industrious habits" and an "aptitude for study," you will finish successfully your course at the academy.

So, unless you have an *unusually brilliant mathematical mind*, do not enter the academy until you have mastered portions of the mathematical studies just mentioned. If your natural capabilities in this line are below the average, do not attempt to enter at all, no matter what your habits are or what you have studied, for you will be sure sooner or later to subject yourself and your friends to "mortification and disappointment."

No matter how brilliant the cadet may be it will be a great advantage to him if, before entering, he has studied a considerable portion of the first year's course, as the majority of cadets discharged for deficiency in studies fail inside of the first year.

It is perfectly immaterial to the Government whether you succeed or fail, for there are plenty of young men waiting to fill your place. All ranks and stations are leveled at the United States Military Academy, and each cadet must stand on his own merits as shown by his individual work, for he will receive no undue credit on account of the rank or prominence of his parents.

To give a tangible idea of the strictness of the examinations, it may be stated in general terms that of all the young men who attempt to pass the entrance examination about one third are rejected.

Of all cadets who succeed in passing this examination over one third are found deficient, and are discharged before completing the four years' course. In other words, only about one third of the young men who receive appointments to West Point succeed in finishing the course and receive commissions in the army.

The foregoing remarks may seem unnecessarily severe and emphatic, but the facts stated certainly justify them. It is hoped that candidates will not be unduly discouraged, for it is better to know the truth before entering than to learn it afterward by hard knocks and sad experience. "Forewarned is forearmed."

Expenses Prior to Entrance.

All expenses of appointees to the Military Academy prior to reporting to the superintendent, June 15th or August 31st, must be borne by the applicant. In the cases of successful candidates, parents are recommended to furnish only sufficient money to cover traveling expenses to the academy.

Character of Entrance Examinations.

The following will give a general idea of the scope of the examination candidates must pass to enter the academy:

Physical Examination.

Every candidate is subjected to a rigid physical examination, and if there is found to exist in him any of the following causes of disqualification to such a degree as would immediately, or at no very distant period, impair his efficiency, he is rejected.

1. Feeble constitution and muscular tenuity; unsound health from whatever cause; indications of former disease; glandular swellings or other symptoms of scrofula.

2. Chronic cutaneous affections, especially of the scalp.

3. Severe injuries of the bones of the head; convulsions.

4. Impaired vision from whatever cause; inflammatory affections of the eyelids; immobility or irregularity of the iris; fistula lachrymalis, etc.

5. Deafness; copious discharge from the ears.

6. Loss of many teeth; or the teeth generally unsound.

7. Impediment of speech.

8. Want of due capacity of the chest, and other indications of a liability to a pulmonic disease.

9. Impaired or inadequate efficiency of one or both of the superior extremities on account of fractures, especially of the clavicle, contraction of a joint, extenuation, deformity, etc.

10. An unusual excurvature or incurvature of the spine.

11. Hernia.

12. A varicose state of the veins of the scrotum or spermatic cord (when large), sarcocele, hydrocele, hæmorrhoids, fistulas.

13. Impaired or inadequate efficiency of one or both of the inferior extremities on account of varicose veins, fractures, malformation (flat feet, etc.), lameness, contraction, unequal length, bunions, overlying or supernumerary toes, etc.

14. Ulcers, or unsound cicatrices of ulcers likely to break out afresh.

Academical Examination.

Reading.—In reading, candidates must be able to read understandingly, with proper accent and emphasis.

Writing and Orthography.—In writing and orthography they must be able, from dictation, to write sentences from standard pieces of English literature, both prose and poetry, sufficient in number to test their qualifications both in handwriting and orthography.

Arithmetic.—In arithmetic they must be able:

1. To explain, accurately and clearly, its objects, and the manner of writing and reading numbers—entire, fractional, compound, or denominate.

2. To perform with facility and accuracy the various operations of addition, subtraction, multiplication, and division of whole numbers, abstract and compound or denominate, giving the rule for each operation, *with its reasons*, and also the different methods of proving the accuracy of the work.

3. To explain the meaning of reduction—its different kinds, its application to denominate numbers in reducing them from a higher to a lower denomination and the reverse, and to equivalent decimals; to give the rule for each case, *with its reasons*, and to apply readily these rules to practical examples of each kind.

4. To explain the nature of prime numbers and factors of a number, of a common divisor of two or more numbers, particularly of their greatest common divisor, with its use, and to give the rule, *with its reasons*, for obtaining it; also the meaning of a common multiple of several numbers, particularly of their least common multiple, and its use, and to give the rule, *with its reasons*, for obtaining it, and to apply each of these rules to examples.

5. To explain the nature of fractions—common or vulgar and decimal; to define the various kinds of fractions, with the distinguishing properties of each; to give all the rules for their reduction, par-

ticularly from mixed to improper and the reverse, from compound to complex or simple, to their lowest terms, to a common denominator, from common to decimal and the reverse; for their addition, subtraction, multiplication, and division, *with the reason* for each change of rule, and to apply each rule to examples.

6. To define the terms *ratio* and *proportion*; to give the properties of proportion and the rules, and their reasons, for stating and solving questions in both simple and compound proportion or single and double rule of three, and to apply these rules to examples.

7. The candidates must not only know the principles and rules referred to above, but they are required to possess such a thorough understanding of all the fundamental operations of arithmetic as will enable them to combine the various principles in the solution of any complex problem which can be solved by methods of arithmetic. In other words, they must possess such a complete knowledge of arithmetic as will enable them to take up at once the higher branches of mathematics without further study of arithmetic.

8. It is to be understood that the examination in these branches may be either written or oral, or

partly written or partly oral; that the definitions and rules must be given fully and accurately; and that the work of all examples, whether upon the blackboard, slate, or paper, must be written plainly and in full, and in such a manner as to show clearly the mode of solution.

The following examples and questions in arithmetic are a few of those which have been used at past examinations; they are given in order to indicate more clearly what is required, and it should be distinctly understood that entirely different ones are used each year.

Multiply 4·32 by ·00012.

Explain the reason for placing the decimal point in the answer (the rule for so doing is not the reason).

Reduce $\dfrac{5\frac{1}{2} + \dfrac{7\frac{1}{4}}{\cdot 5} - 0\cdot 725}{\dfrac{4 + 3\cdot 45}{2\frac{1}{2}}}$ to an equivalent decimal.

Divide 3380321 by MDCCXCIX, and express the quotient by the Roman system of notation.

Change ·013 to an equivalent fraction whose denominator is 135.

Find the greatest common divisor of $26\frac{1}{4}$, $28\frac{3}{8}$, and $29\frac{1}{4}$.

How many men would be required to cultivate a field of $2\frac{5}{8}$ acres in $5\frac{1}{2}$ days of 10 hours each, if each man completed 77 square yards in 9 hours?

Separate $772\frac{2}{3}$ into three numbers which shall be in the same proportion as $2\frac{1}{2}$, $\frac{7}{10}$, $\frac{6}{10}$.

Five cubic feet of gold weigh 98·20 times as much as a cubic foot of water, and 2 cubic feet of copper weigh 18 times as much as a cubic foot of water: how many cubic feet of copper will weigh as much as $\frac{7}{8}$ of a cubic inch of gold?

Find the least common multiple for the numbers $\frac{3}{4}$, 2·1, 5·25, $\frac{7}{8}$.

A wins 9 games out of 15 when playing against B, and 16 out of 25 when playing against C: how many games out of the 118 should C win playing against B?

A and B run a race, their rates of running being as 17 to 18; A runs $2\frac{1}{4}$ miles in 16 minutes 48 seconds, and B runs the entire distance in 34 minutes: what was the entire distance?

A and B can do a piece of work in 4 hours, A and C in $3\frac{2}{3}$ hours, B and C in $5\frac{1}{4}$ hours: in what time can A do it alone?

English shillings are coined from a metal which contains 37 parts of silver to 3 parts of alloy; 1 pound of this metal is coined into 66 shillings.

The United States silver dollar weighs 412·5 grains, and consists of 9 parts silver to 1 of alloy. What fraction of the United States dollar will contain the same amount of silver as one English shilling?

Give the rule for reducing a decimal of a given denomination to integers of lower denominations.

What is the effect of dividing the denominator of a fraction by a whole number, and why?

Explain the difference between a common fraction and a decimal.

What is the effect of annexing a cipher to a decimal, and why?

If the same number be subtracted from both terms of an improper fraction, what will be the effect? Why?

Give the rule for reducing a common fraction to an equivalent decimal, and explain why the resulting decimal will be equal to the common fraction from which it is obtained.

Give the rule for dividing one decimal by another, and explain why the decimal point in the quotient is placed where the rule directs.

Define reduction, and state the different kinds.

Grammar. — In English grammar candidates must be able:

1. To define the parts of speech, and give their

classes and properties; to give inflections, including declension, conjugation, and comparison; to give the corresponding masculine and feminine gender nouns; to give and apply the ordinary rules of syntax.

2. To parse fully and correctly any ordinary sentence, omitting rules, declensions, comparisons, and principal parts, but giving the subject of each verb, the governing word of each objective case, the word for which each pronoun stands or to which it refers, the words between which each preposition shows the relation, precisely what each conjunction connects, what each adjective and adverb qualifies or limits, the construction of each infinitive, and, generally, showing a good knowledge of the function of each word in the sentence. Omissions will be taken to indicate ignorance.

3. To correct in sentences or extracts any ordinary grammatical errors, such as are mentioned and explained in ordinary grammars.

It is not required that any particular grammarian or text-book shall be followed; but rules, definitions, parsing, and corrections must be in accordance with good usage and common sense. The examinations may be written or oral, or both written and oral.

Geography.—Candidates will be required to pass a satisfactory examination, written or oral, or both, in geography, particularly of our own country. To give the candidate a clear idea of what is required, the following synopsis is added to show the character and extent of the examination. Questions are likely to be asked involving the knowledge of:

1. Definitions of geographical circles, of latitude and longitude, of zones, and of all the natural divisions of the earth's surface, as islands, seas, capes, etc.

2. The continental areas and grand divisions of the water of the earth's surface.

3. The grand divisions of the land—the large bodies of water which in part or wholly surround them.

Their principal mountains, location, direction, and extent; the capes, from what parts they project and into what waters.

Their principal peninsulas, location, and by what waters they are embraced.

The parts connected by an isthmus, if any.

Their principal islands, location, and surrounding waters.

The seas, gulfs, and bays, the coasts they indent, and the waters to which they are subordinate.

The straits, the lands they separate, and the waters they connect.

Their principal rivers, their sources, directions of flow, and the waters into which they empty.

Their principal lakes, location, and extent.

4. The political divisions of the grand divisions.

Their names, locations, boundaries, and capitals; general questions of the same character as indicated in the second section made applicable to each of the countries of each of the grand divisions.

5. The United States.

The candidate should be thoroughly informed as to its general features, configuration, location, and boundaries (both with respect to neighboring countries and latitude and longitude); its adjacent oceans, seas, bays, gulfs, sounds, straits, and islands; its mountain ranges, their location and extent; the sources, directions, and terminations of the important rivers and their principal tributaries; the lakes, and, in short, every geographical feature of the country as indicated above. The location and termination of important railroad lines and other means of communication from one part of the country to another should not be omitted.

The States and Territories are to be accurately located with respect to each other by their boundaries, and as to their order along the Atlantic coast, the Gulf of Mexico, the Pacific coast, the northern frontier, the Mexican frontier, and the Mississippi, Missouri, and Ohio Rivers.

The boundary and other large rivers of each State, as well as all other prominent geographical features, should be known.

The names and locations of their capitals, and other important cities and towns, are likewise to be known.

In short, the knowledge should be so complete that a clear mental picture of the whole or any part of the United States is impressed on the mind of the candidate. More weight is attached to a knowledge of the geography of the United States than to that of all other countries combined.

History.—The candidate should make himself familiar with so much of the history of the United States as is contained in the ordinary school histories. The examination may be written or oral, or partly written and partly oral, and will usually consist of a series of questions similar to the following:

1. When, where, and by whom were the original thirteen colonies settled, and what were the different kinds of government in each prior to the Revolution?

2. Various wars both before and after the Revolution, their causes, prominent generals, and battles in each. Results of each war.

3. The Presidents of the United States in their order, and the leading events in the administration of each.

4. The Constitution of the United States, why formed, and when adopted; powers in different branches of Congress, qualifications and manner of electing its members.

5. Election and qualifications of the President, and his powers. Passage of bills, etc.

Points in Regard to the Entrance Examination.

A general average of about seventy-five per cent is required, and no candidate having an average in any one subject of less than sixty-five per cent will be accepted.

It will be noted that the time given to each subject is limited, so that if in doubt as to a question or problem, after due thought, it is best to number the question in its proper place, leaving a blank space with a view to solving the problem later, and go on and finish the answers to the questions which you are reasonably sure will be correct. Then, if time permits, go back to the doubtful points and attempt to solve them.

Always write your *number* and place of examination on each separate sheet of paper. Number your questions and answers in their order, leaving a margin of about an inch on the left-hand side of each page. Make your answers clear and concise, writing legibly and grammatically, for your examination papers may be considered in determining your proficiency in writing, grammar, and spelling. Communicating with your neighbor or "cribbing" is alone cause for rejection.

Number each separate sheet of paper consecutively, beginning with the first, and, if time permits, after completing an examination, read over the questions to see that you have not misunderstood any of them. Go over your work carefully and correct any errors that may have crept in. You can not be too particular with a written examination.

Many institutions in this country admit students upon certificates or diplomas received from other schools, but such is not the case at the Military Academy. Every candidate must pass the prescribed examination, and, if successful, he is required to take a full four-years' course, no matter how many diplomas or certificates he may possess. So it will be useless to present such papers to the examining board. There are, however, several schools in the vicinity of West Point that make a special business of preparing candidates for the entrance examination, and in many instances money thus spent on a candidate has proved to be well invested.

When and where the Examinations are held.

Boards for the examination of appointees to the United States Military Academy are convened March 1st and July 15th annually, at military posts nearest the following cities—viz., Boston, New York city or West Point, Baltimore, Columbus, Ohio, Atlanta, New Orleans, San Antonio, Chicago, St. Louis, Leavenworth, Kan., Omaha, Keogh, Mont., Cheyenne, San Francisco, San Diego, and Vancouver. Candidates will be directed to appear for mental and physical examination at the military post nearest their respective places of residence, and no candidate will be permitted to appear for examination at any other time or place than that specified in his instructions from the War Department. A candidate who fails *physically* will not be examined mentally.

As soon as the preliminary examination is concluded, each candidate repairs to his home and awaits the notification of the result of his examination, which will be sent from the War Department as soon as practicable.

In order to insure impartiality, the examination questions are prepared at West Point and sent to the different boards under seal. The board takes the name of each candidate and gives to him a number, which he places on all his examination papers, *never putting his name* on them. The numbers and corresponding names are immediately sent to the War Department. Upon the completion of the examination, the papers are sent direct to the superintendent of the Military Academy, where they are examined by the academic board. The results of the examination are then sent to the War Department by simply *stating* the number of each successful candidate and place of examination. The War Department then finds the names corresponding to the successful *numbers*, and issues directions for the successful candidates to report to the superintendent of the academy June 15th or August 31st, depending on the date of examination.

The New Cadet.

Having been duly notified by the War Department that you have passed the entrance examination, you will be directed to report at the academy on a certain date, June 15th or August 31st, depending upon whether you were examined in March or July. Make such arrangements as will cause you to arrive at West Point on the morning of the day you are directed to report. Upon arrival, report at once to the adjutant of the academy. He will receive you kindly and have you assigned to quarters without delay, so that you will be at no unnecessary expense after arrival.

Do not burden your trunk with a supply of useless clothing, pictures, bric-a-brac, etc. A year's supply of underclothing, a few white shirts, collars, cuffs, a dozen towels, the usual toilet articles, and one good suit of clothes will be all the personal effects you need. Civilian clothing, pictures, ornaments, etc., are not allowed in your room, so such things will be utterly useless. All other necessary articles can be obtained at the academy, of uniform pattern and moderate in price.

If you are homesick it will soon wear off. Love sickness is more dangerous, but rest assured at so young an age it is only "puppy" love, and will readily die a natural death. You may have similar attacks while at the academy or "on furlough," but they should be strangled at your earliest convenience.

Give your relatives and friends to understand that it is a court-martial offense for a new cadet to have any one visit him at the academy. A new cadet or "plebe" is literally "out of sight," and he should avoid embarrassment by discouraging his friends from trying to see him. Have them wait until the end of your first year, when you become a bold, dashing "yearling," and you will then have time to give them a hearty welcome in "Yearling Camp."

If you have received previous military training it will be of great advantage to you. At all events, do not be discouraged. Start in with a determination to be honorable, respectful to your seniors, prompt and cheerful in the obedience of all lawful orders. Never attempt to argue a point, or dispute the correctness or legality of an order, for experience will teach you that it is probably all right even if you fail to see it. Remember also that there are no such words as *can't* and *won't* in a soldier's vocabulary.

You may meet with many new and weird experiences, but stand up and take them like a man, and you will be honored and respected by your comrades. If, however, your honor or your self-respect be called in question, protect them at all hazards.

Learn to think for yourself, and think long and hard before asking assistance. In your studies you will find that explanations from your instructors are expensive luxuries. It is related that every smile or explanation granted a cadet lowers his mark about twenty per cent; and, moreover, it gives the instructor the advantage of you by helping him to "size you up" in reporting your abilities to the academic board.

Above all, come to a "realizing sense of your inferiority" as soon as practicable. Work hard, and secure a high standing in your class at the end of the first six months, for after this period transfers are few and far between, and then with due application you should be able to hold your ground. It is hard to rise after the class is once fairly arranged, but if you get started downward the odds are against you; and it seems as if every one is waiting to give you a push in that direction. It is rumored also that while the maximum mark in the first section is three units, in the lowest section of the class (the "immortals") it is but 2·5 units. Moral: Keep out of the "immortals."

Should you stand low in your class, press on, do your best, remembering that many of our most noted generals have graduated near the bottom of their classes. It is sometimes said that it takes a smarter man to stand at the bottom of his class than it does to graduate at the head of it. Even should you fail to graduate do not grieve about it, although it does pain and surprise your friends. The brightest minds are not always found in brilliant mathematicians. Cadets found deficient and discharged are sometimes head and shoulders the mental and physical superiors of some who graduate. You will yet succeed in life if you are made of the right kind of material. A masterly retreat shows as much ability as a hard-earned victory.

Pay of Cadets.

The pay of a cadet is forty-five dollars per month, to commence with his admission into the academy, and is sufficient, with proper economy, for his support. No cadet is permitted to receive money or other supplies from any person whomsoever without the sanction of the superintendent. Four dollars per month are retained from the pay of each cadet, so that upon graduation he will have saved about $190, which will go toward the purchase of his uniform and equipments as a commissioned officer.

The pay is not actually turned over to the cadet each month, but he has what is known as a " check " or account book, upon which is entered each month the amount of his pay. From this is deducted the cost of his board, washing, clothing, text-books, etc., and the balance is carried forward to the next month. The clothing is furnished and the washing done by the academy at the lowest possible figure. The cadets all board at the mess hall, an establishment fitted with all modern improvements and under the immediate charge of an army officer, who manages it in an orderly and economical manner. The entire cost of running the mess hall is divided *pro rata* among the cadets, the board of each ranging from fifteen to eighteen dollars per month. The food is excellent in quality, sufficient in quantity, and surpasses in cleanliness and variety that of any similar establishment in this country.

The tuition is absolutely free, but parents are required to deposit with the treasurer of the academy about one hundred dollars upon their son's entrance, which sum is placed to his credit to cover the expense of his first outfit of uniform, bedding, and books. No money should be sent to a cadet unless for very urgent reasons previously approved by the superintendent. He has no use for money, and can spend it only at places and for purposes prohibited by the regulations of the academy. Other necessary supplies may be sent on approval, but cadets wear no jewelry, and eatables must be taken to the mess hall and regularly served.

The pay of each cadet for the months of July and August of his second year is given to him in advance, and may be used by him during his two months' furlough which is granted at that time.

At the end of the four-years' course, upon graduation, graduates are given their retained pay and all money saved by them from their regular pay as shown by the balance on their account books.

Length of Service in the Army.

In the Appendix will be found the articles of agreement into which a cadet enters, binding him to serve in the army for at least eight years, unless sooner discharged. Also his oath of allegiance to uphold and defend the Constitution, and to serve the United States against all its enemies whomsoever. In time of peace, however, the resignation of a cadet or an officer is always accepted, so that in reality he can close his military career at any desired period. In time of war or great public danger his services might be needed, and he would then doubtless be required to fulfill his engagement.

Although a West Point education fits a man for almost any walk in life, very few choose to throw off the yoke of a soldier to take up some other profession. The average graduate leaves his old iron Alma Mater with a high sense of honor, manly in deportment, and well grounded in the profession of arms. He has lost touch with the friends of his youth, his sweethearts are all married, the old schoolhouse and other familiar landmarks seem to have shrunk in size and importance. In short, all seems changed, and he is imbued with the one idea of joining his regiment and continuing his life as a soldier.

Academic Duties.

The academic duties and exercises commence on the 1st of September and continue until about the middle of June. Examinations of the several classes are held in January and June, and at the former such of the new cadets as are found proficient in studies and conduct are given the particular standing in their classes to which their merits entitle them. After either examination cadets found deficient in studies or conduct are discharged and sent to their homes, unless for special reasons in each case the academic board should otherwise recommend. The traveling expenses of cadets discharged in this manner are paid by the Government. The expenses of cadets who resign or who are dismissed are not paid by the Government. Similar examinations are held every January and June during the four years comprising the course of study. These examinations are very thorough, and require from the cadet a close and persevering attention to study, without evasion or slighting of any part of the course, as no relaxation of any kind is made by the examiners.

It seems unnecessary, in a book of this character, to go into the details of the work required of each class. A good general idea of the requirements of each year may be had by referring to the Appendix, where the course of study pursued is given in tabulated form, and by noting the following cursory review of the average cadet's career. The various and multitudinous regulations and customs of the academy will be grasped gradually as the cadet advances in his career, and it does not seem expedient to attempt to elucidate them in a volume of this scope.

The first two months (July and August) are spent in camp, when studying is tabooed, all time being devoted to his preliminary practical military training. This is known as "Plebe" Camp. Here he is drilled in infantry and foot artillery, and when sufficiently advanced is introduced to his duties as a sentinel on guard both day and night. If he has had any previous training in this line it will be greatly to his advantage, for there is so much to learn that is entirely new that his life may seem more or less of a burden to him, for it is all work and no play to the new cadet. In fact, the life of a cadet at the academy for the first year is a series of hard knocks, but in the end they bear good fruit. In the past ten years the custom of *hazing* has disappeared. Many new cadets will think, doubtless, that the discipline is so strict that hazing could not add much to their burdens. To many of the older graduates the system of hazing seems to be a good thing, and they are of the opinion that the discipline of the academy is on the wane since it was abolished. In fact, hazing would be a good thing if the line could be drawn at a certain point; but as it could not be, it was decided to cut out the custom, root and branch.

In September the new cadet goes to the barracks, settles down to work—and hard work, too, will he find it—for the remainder of the year; but if he possesses the capacity and habits already commented upon, he will probably pull through to the following June, when he will have—a vacation? Not at all. He will find himself in camp again doing guard duty, drilling, "learning how to sleep on the ground," and wondering when those new cadets will get enough beaten into their heads to go on guard and make it easier for him. In the vernacular of the academy this is called "Yearling" Camp.

During this encampment, however, it will not be all work to the average cadet; he will be permitted to go to the weekly hops which take place every summer. He can get a pass occasionally to leave camp and meander down "Flirtation Walk," see the boats go by, and possibly meet his "cousin," who will assist him by her interesting ways to enjoy his gorgeous surroundings.

September finds him hard at work on the second year's course. Pleasure is discarded, for the studies this year are really more difficult than those in the first year, but he has learned how to study and how to recite, so his work is no harder than before.

Successfully passing his January and June examinations, he is exultant:

> " For the furlough has come,
> For two months he'll be free
> From the deuced reveille,
> And the boom of the evening gun."

During the months of July and August of this year he is released from all duties at the academy, and may spend his time where he chooses.

The realization of this short vacation, coupled with its anticipation, is next to the most important and enjoyable event in a cadet's career. For two long years he has been confined at hard work to this small but lovely military spot. He returns promptly the last of August, climbing the well-known hill, grip and cane in hand, silk hat crowning all, which, by the way, will be torn or kicked into samples by his gray-coated comrades on the hill. September 1st finds him pinned down to his room in the old gray barracks, where he " bones " away on the third year's course. This year's course will be more interesting to him than either of the two that has gone before, but to succeed he will find he must remember all he has learned in the first two years, as direct application of it is made in this as well as in the following year, and he will not have time to turn to the calculus to find out what the author of his "phil" means by saying, "By differentiating this expression we *easily* get *this* expression."

Having finished philosophy and chemistry, he heaves a sigh of relief, and June finds him in camp again as a first classman and only one more year to stay. During this encampment his military work is of a much higher order, being usually on duty as a cadet officer and engaged in helping to instruct the other cadets as well as learning practical lessons himself of a higher nature. He feels the dignity of his position, attends the summer hops, flirts with the charming damsels who visit the post at this season, and enjoys generally what is termed "First Class" Camp. He looks with more or less pity on the "plebes" and "yearlings," who have only just commenced their military careers, remembering the while that this is his last camp at the academy.

Camp is "broken," and he returns to barracks and academic buildings with a strong heart for study, as he is now on the "home stretch," and his commission is in sight. He is hardened to work by this time, and moves along with his daily duties with apparent ease. As the following spring opens and the ice-bound Hudson breaks her chains his studies seem to grow harder, and he longs to break away and join the birds in their frolics, but the end is too near now to give way to such idle thoughts. Then comes graduation, when he "doffs the cadet and dons the brevet," for in his hand he holds his hard-earned diploma and an appointment as a second lieutenant in the regular army.

It may appear from this rapid sketch that the life of a cadet is one of continual study, with but little rest or recreation during the four years. In the main this appearance is a reality, for the only time a cadet is allowed to leave the academy is during the two months at the close of his second year, and possibly two or three days at Christmas. Recitations or drills take place every day of the year, Sundays and national holidays excepted.

The only time a cadet has to himself is a portion of Saturday afternoon and evening, about half an hour after each meal, and during the winter months about an hour before supper. Sunday morning he reluctantly goes to chapel, and Sunday afternoon and evening he spends preparing Monday's lessons. He rises at 6 A. M. and retires at 10 P. M. each day.

His drills and gymnasium work afford him sufficient bodily exercise, and in the past year he seems to have employed his spare time Saturdays playing baseball and football. But it may be relied on that unless the course of study is very much modified the average cadet will not have time to engage in these games, as is done at many colleges, without losing ground in his classes, to say the least; for there is more hard studying and more thorough work of all kinds accomplished at the academy than at any other institution in this country in the same space of time.

During the months of July and August of each year all cadets except the "furlough class" live in camp, which is given up to practical work in the line of the military profession; besides the regular drills and guard duty, the cadets learn and practice much that pertains to the life of a soldier in actual campaign.

Assignments after Graduation.

When a cadet shall receive a regular degree from the academic board, after going through the classes, he is considered as among the candidates for a commission in the engineer corps, artillery, infantry, or cavalry, according to the duties he may be judged competent to perform. As a rule, the cadets choose the particular arm of the service and regiment or corps according to their class standing at graduation. The first three or four are assigned to the engineer corps, about the next ten choose the artillery, and the remainder choose cavalry or infantry. Formerly some regiments were considered more desirable than others, as there was more chance for promotion in them, but now that promotion is lineal instead of regimental no regiment possesses any real advantages over another. Some have better stations than others, but regiments change station every few years, and in the end each enjoys its share of good stations.

Graduates for whom there are no vacancies in the army are commissioned additional second lieutenants, receiving the pay and allowances of second lieutenants until vacancies do exist. So that all who graduate are eventually sure of their commissions as second lieutenants.

Join your station in due time, and go to the adjutant's office after guard mounting of the day you are directed to report. Appear in proper uniform, and with soldierly bearing present your order of assignment to the regimental adjutant and report to him for duty. After being formally presented to the commanding officer, report to the quartermaster for assignment to quarters. You should already have provided yourself with furnishings for a bedroom.

As soon as possible after reporting, you should make formal calls upon your commanding officer and upon the captain of your company at their respective quarters. Rather than confine your conversation to West Point topics, talk about the weather.

If you are married, leave your wife at home, or in the nearest town, until you can provide a suitable home for her. A newly fledged second lieutenant is very much like a "plebe" at the academy, and he will be much better off without a wife until he has had a little experience in his new sphere of life.

Remember also that the men in your company are not "plebes," but are more like children, and should be treated kindly but firmly, in order that their respect and confidence may be gained as well as their obedience. Even should your first sergeant be disposed to give you "points," do not put him in arrest for disrespect, for it is quite possible that your captain would rather dispense with your services than with those of his first sergeant. Gradually you will convince the first sergeant that you know a thing or two; but do not imagine that you know it all, for you will soon learn that your captain, and even the first sergeant, know more than you thought they did.

FROM THE MILITARY ACADEMY.

The following copies of the questions at the entrance examination held at West Point in June, 1886, will give the candidate a fair idea of what may be required at future examinations:

EXAMINATION IN ARITHMETIC.

1. What decimal fraction, multiplied by 175, will be equal to the sum of ¼, 1⅜, 4⅞, and 3½?

2. How many miles will a plowman walk in plowing an acre if each furrow is one foot in width?

3. If $29\frac{147}{8765} \times \frac{7952}{\cdot 00004}$ be subtracted from each of the two numbers $475\frac{17}{19}$ and 2·10009, will the ratio of the two remainders, taken in order, be the same as that of the two numbers? Why?

4. On a centigrade thermometer the freezing point is zero, and the boiling point is 100°. On a Fahrenheit thermometer the freezing point is 32°, and the boiling point is 212°. What degree on a centigrade corresponds to 68° Fahrenheit?

5. How many pounds of tea are equivalent to 10½ pounds of butter, when 5 pounds of tea are equivalent to 14 pounds of coffee; 9 of coffee to 20

of sugar; 10 of sugar to 6 of cheese; and 10 of cheese to 9 of butter?

6. If $44\frac{1}{2}$ guineas weigh one pound Troy, and 32 half-pennies weigh one pound avoirdupois, what is the difference, in grains, between the weights of a guinea and a half-penny?

7. Twenty-one thousand dollars is to be divided among A, B, C, and D. A's share is to B's as $2:3$, B's to C's as $4:5$, C's to D's as $6:7$. What will each receive?

8. If 30 men working 11 hours a day can do a piece of work in a certain time, how many more must be employed when it is half done in order to finish it in the same time, all working 10 hours a day on the last half?

9. The value of a pound of gold is 14 times that of a pound of silver, and the weights of bars of equal size of gold and silver are as $19:10$. Find the value of a bar of silver equal in size to a bar of gold worth £1,750.

EXAMINATION IN WRITING AND ORTHOGRAPHY.

Write and punctuate the following:

It was not only by the efficiency of the restraints imposed on the royal prerogative that England was advantageously distinguished from most of the neighboring countries. A peculiarity equally important, though less noticed, was the relation in which the nobility stood here to the commonalty. There was a strong hereditary aristocracy, but it was of all hereditary aristocracies the least insolent and exclusive. It had none of the invidious characters of a caste. It was constantly receiving members from the people and constantly sending down members to mingle with the people. Any gentleman might become a peer. A younger son of a peer was but a gentleman. Grandsons of peers yielded precedence to newly made knights. The dignity of knighthood was not beyond the reach of any man who could by diligence and thrift realize a good estate, or who could attract notice by his valor in a battle or siege. It was regarded as no disparagement for the daughter of a duke, nay, of a royal duke, to espouse a distinguished commoner.

> His was the pomp, the crowded hall,
>   But where is now his proud display?
> His riches, honors, pleasures—all
>   Desire could frame; but where are they?
> And he, as some tall rock that stands,
>   Protected by the circling sea,
> Surrounded by admiring bands,
>   Seemed proudly strong—and where is he?

Spelling.

1. Agility.	13. Coliseum.
2. Annular.	14. Collide.
3. Antecedent.	15. Dalliance.
4. Artillery.	16. Debarred.
5. Ascend.	17. Deceive.
6. Barbarism.	18. Exhibit.
7. Barricade.	19. Exonerate.
8. Bigotry.	20. Fascinate.
9. Bounteous.	21. Grammar.
10. College.	22. Irritate.
11. Communicate.	23. Menace.
12. Coherence.	24. Parallel.

EXAMINATION IN ENGLISH GRAMMAR.
(Time allotted: two and one half hours.)

Division I.

(N. B.—Write the answers below, numbering them to correspond with the questions.)

1. What is declension? Decline child, who, he.
2. Write the plural of dwarf, fly, pen, ox, footman, calf, handful, cargo, chimney, potato.
3. What is a sentence? Name the different kinds of sentences. What is a phrase? What is a

clause? Give examples of the sentence, the phrase, and the clause.

4. What is a conjunction? How do you parse a conjunction?

5. What is an adjective? Of what inflection or change of form do adjectives admit?

Division II.

(N. B.—Write quite across both pages, if necessary. In parsing, give no rules, declensions, or principal parts; but in other respects parse fully, being careful to give the subject of each verb, the governing word of each objective case, and to state precisely what each conjunction connects, between what words each preposition shows the relation, and to what each pronoun refers. Important omissions will be taken to indicate ignorance. Intelligible abbreviations are allowed.)

Parse the words in italics in the following sentence: *In* free States *no man* should take up arms *but with* a view *to defend* his country and its laws; he *puts off* the citizen *when* he enters the camp; *but it* is *because* he is a *citizen* and would continue *such* that he makes *himself for* a *while* a *soldier.*

Division III.

Correct all errors in the following sentences, including bad arrangement of words:

1. His work is one of the best that has been published.
2. No Roman emperor was so cruel nor so tyrannical as Nero.
3. Have you no other excuse but this?
4. We not only obtained Louisiana, but Florida also, by purchase.
5. Flour will not do to make our bread alone.
6. The number of inhabitants were not more than four millions.
7. They told me of him having failed.
8. But she fell a laughing like one out of their right mind.
9. What else could he do in the circumstances he was placed?
10. Whom do you suppose it was?
11. The board of directors looked gravely; in fact, a frown began to settle on its face.
12. Why have you not kept the promise you have made when I was at your house?
13. Suppose Xerxes had have succeeded in conquering Greece!

14. If I were in his place, I would not have gone.

15. These flowers smell sweetly and look beautifully.

16. There is no charity in giving of money to the intemperate.

17. I have and ever shall insist on the necessity of economy.

18. The dahlia, as well as the fuschia, is a native of America.

19. The spirit and not the letter of the law, are what we are to follow.

20. London is the largest of any city in Europe.

21. Am I the scholar who am to be punished?

22. The man could neither read or write.

23. Every one of your arguments are absurd.

Examination in History.

(Time allotted: three hours.)

1. Name the first discoverer of America from each of the following countries, and give the date of each discovery:

(1) England.

(2) Spain.

(3) France.

2. Write after each of the following-named colo-

nies the date and locality of the first settlement, and state to what nation the settlers belonged:

(1) Georgia.

(2) Maryland.

(3) Pennsylvania.

(4) Virginia.

3. When, and as the result of what war, were the French possessions in Canada transferred to England?

4. What were the boundaries of the territories of the United States after the close of the Revolutionary War?

(1) North.

(2) South.

(3) East.

(4) West.

5. When and where did each of the following events occur?

(1) The first colonial Congress.

(2) Burgoyne's surrender.

(3) Arnold's treason.

6. Name two defects in the Articles of Confederation which made it necessary to form a new Constitution for the United States.

7. When and where was the first Government organized under the present Constitution?

8. Under whose administration did each of the following events occur?

(1) The Louisiana purchase.

(2) The Nullification act.

(3) The Missouri Compromise.

(4) The Gadsden purchase.

9. When and from whom was the territory acquired which is comprised in each of the following-named States?

(1) Texas.

(2) California.

(3) Florida.

(4) Arizona.

10. Name three States of the Union which have been admitted since the adoption of the Federal Constitution, and which belonged, wholly or in part, to other States of the Union.

11. Name the States in the Union in which slavery existed in 1861.

12. Which of the slave States passed the ordinance of secession, and which remained loyal to the Government at Washington?

13. Give the names, dates, and immediate results of six important battles of the civil war.

14. What text-books in United States history have you studied?

Examination in Geography.

1. What proportion of the earth's surface is land?

2. Which hemisphere contains the more land, northern or southern?

3. If one should start from a point on the equator in the mid-Atlantic and travel eastward entirely around the earth, keeping on the equator, name the bodies of land and water over which he would pass.

4. Name the five largest oceans of the earth.

5. Name all the States and Territories of the United States which touch the Atlantic, the Pacific, or the Gulf of Mexico.

6. Name the States east of the Mississippi which touch neither the Gulf of Mexico, the Atlantic, nor the Great Lakes.

7. Bound the following States and Territories: Idaho, Arizona, Indian Territory, Minnesota, Kentucky, North Carolina, and Vermont.

8. What States and Territories lie, in part or wholly, west of the Rocky Mountain system?

9. Locate definitely the following places, stating upon what waters they are situated: Montgomery, Macon, Shreveport, Little Rock, Austin, Albuquer-

que, Sacramento, Cheyenne, Detroit, Harrisburg, Bangor, Milwaukee.

10. If a man should start from Santa Fé and go due north to the British line, through what States and Territories would he pass?

11. The parallel of St. Louis, between the Atlantic and the Pacific, passes through what States and Territories?

12. What political divisions of South America, between its most easterly and southerly points, border on the Atlantic Ocean?

13. In going from St. Petersburg to Bombay by steamer, nearest route, over what waters and by what countries would you pass?

14. What countries of Europe touch Austria?

15. Where is Beloochistan?

16. Where is Nankin? upon what water is it situated?

17. What is the general direction of the Hoang-Ho or Yellow River? where does it empty?

18. Where is Cambodia? to what country does it belong?

19. Where is the Gulf of Salonica?

20. Where is the Strait of Otranto?

CHAPTER II.

COMMISSIONS FROM THE RANKS OF THE REGULAR ARMY.

As stated at the beginning of Chapter I, existing laws and regulations state that vacancies in the grade of second lieutenant are filled by appointment from the graduates of the Military Academy, so long as any such remain in service unassigned. Vacancies thereafter are filled by appointment of competitors from the army favorably recommended under act of Congress approved June 30, 1892. This act of Congress, and the rules prescribed by the War Department for the examination of competitors, are given in detail in the following order:

HEADQUARTERS OF THE ARMY,
ADJUTANT-GENERAL'S OFFICE,
Washington, November 26, 1892.

GENERAL ORDERS, No. 79.

By direction of the Secretary of War the following law, and the regulations established by the

President to carry the same into effect, are published for the information and guidance of all concerned:

Be it enacted by the Senate and House of Representatives of the United States of America in Congress assembled, That the President be, and he is hereby, authorized to prescribe a system of examination of enlisted men of the army, by such boards as may be established by him, to determine their fitness for promotion to the grade of second lieutenant: *Provided,* That all unmarried soldiers under thirty years of age, who are citizens of the United States, are physically sound, who have served honorably not less than two years in the army, and who have borne a good moral character before and after enlistment, may compete for promotion under any system authorized by this act.

SEC. 2. That the members and recorder of such boards as may be established by the President, under the provisions of the preceding section, shall be sworn in every case to discharge their duties honestly and faithfully; and the boards may examine witnesses, and take depositions, for which purposes they shall have such powers of a court of inquiry as may be necessary.

SEC. 3. That the vacancies in the grade of second lieutenant heretofore filled by the promotion of meritorious noncommissioned officers of the army, under the provisions of section three of the act approved June eighteenth, eighteen hundred and seventy-eight, shall be filled by the appointment of competitors favorably recommended under this act, in the order of merit established by the final examination. Each man who passes the final examination shall receive a certificate of eligibility, setting forth the subjects in which he is proficient and the especial grounds upon which the recommendation is based: *Provided*, That not more than two examinations shall be accorded to the same competitor.

Sec. 4. That all rights and privileges arising from a certificate of eligibility may be vacated by sentence of a court-martial; but no soldier, while holding the privileges of a certificate, shall be brought before a garrison or regimental court-martial or summary court.

Sec. 5. That sections three and four of the act approved June eighteenth, eighteen hundred and seventy-eight, providing for the promotion of meritorious noncommissioned officers, be, and the same are hereby, repealed.

Approved July 30, 1892.

I. For the purpose of computing age and length of service, the first day of September of each year, commencing with 1893, is fixed as the date of competition.

Any soldier, otherwise qualified, whose age will not exceed thirty years on the first of September following, and who shall have served honorably not less than two years in the army, on or before that date, may (on or before the first day of February of any year after 1892) make application, through the regular military channels, to his department commander, for preliminary examination, with a view to determine his eligibility for entering the competitive examinations.

PRELIMINARY EXAMINATION.

II. As soon as practicable after the fifteenth of March the department commander will convene a board of five commissioned officers, including two medical officers, for the preliminary examination of applicants, and will order the applicants in his command to appear before it. This board will institute a rigid inquiry into the character, capacity, record, and qualifications of the several candidates, and will recommend none for competitive examination who are not able to establish their fitness for promotion to the entire satisfaction of the board. To that end the procedure of the department boards will be based upon that of retiring boards. Evidence will be obtained from the certificates of officers, from witnesses, under oath, and by means of sworn interrogatories. The military record of each candidate will be closely examined, and his antecedents before entering the service will be made the subject of special inquiry.

Every applicant will be subjected to a rigid physical examination, and if there be found to exist any cause of disqualification to such a degree as might in the future impair his efficiency as an officer in the army, he will be rejected. Examination as to physical qualifications shall conform to the standard required of recruits, and a certificate of physical examination by the medical officers of the board shall accompany the proceedings of the board.

The preliminary examination will embrace the following subjects:

1. English grammar, including orthography, reading, and writing from oral dictation.

2. Mathematics, including arithmetic, algebra, to include the solution of equations of the first degree containing one unknown quantity, the use of loga-

rithms, the elements of plane geometry, plane trigonometry, and surveying.

3. Geography, particularly in reference to the United States and North America.

4. The outlines of general history, and particularly the history of the United States.

5. The Constitution of the United States and the organization of the Government under it, and the elements of international law.

6. Army regulations, and the drill regulations of the arm from which he is selected. The examination in drill regulations will be practical, extending through the schools of the soldier, squad, and platoon, and shall take place on the parade-ground in the presence of the board.

7. The military record of the candidates as certified to by their company, post, and regimental commanders.

8. Physical aptitude, as determined by the medical examination; proficiency in athletics, skill in field sports, etc.

9. Moral character and civil record as verified by the investigations of the board.

In awarding marks, the board will give to each subject in the examination the relative weight given in the following example. The weight to be given to each question will be determined by its importance, and will be set opposite the question in the papers furnished the candidates:

Example.

1. English grammar, orthography, etc............. 100
2. Mathematics................................. 200
3. Geography................................... 100
4. History...................................... 100
5. Constitution and international law............. 100
6. Army and drill regulations and military capacity and aptitude as determined therefrom....... 200
7. Military record............................... 100
8. Physique..................................... 100
9. Moral character and antecedents............... 200

                                                1,200

The duty of making the preliminary examination of applicants is one involving, in a high degree, the welfare and character of the service, and all officers of departmental boards are enjoined to exercise the utmost circumspection and care, not only that no unworthy applicant be recommended, but also that the most worthy shall be recommended. All statements and certificates as to moral character, general aptitude and fitness, should be carefully verified by disinterested evidence.

Separate records will be submitted in each case to the department commander, who will forward them, with all papers presented in relation to the applicant, to the adjutant-general of the army.

COMPETITIVE EXAMINATION.

III. A board to consist of five commissioned officers (including two medical officers, whose duties will be confined to inquiring into and reporting upon the physical qualifications of the applicants) will be convened by the War Department, to meet at Fort Leavenworth, Kansas, on the 1st of September of each year, commencing with 1893, to conduct the final competitive examination of the applicants who have successfully passed the departmental boards, in conformity with the following regulations:

IV. Every applicant will be subjected to a rigid physical examination, and if there be found to exist any cause of disqualification to such a degree as might in the future impair his efficiency as an officer in the army, he will be rejected. Examination as to physical qualifications shall conform to the standard required of recruits, and shall include a certificate of physical examination by the medical officers of the board to accompany the proceedings of the board.

The board, being satisfied as to these preliminary

points, will proceed to examine each candidate separately in the following subjects:

1. English grammar, including orthography, reading, and writing from oral dictation.

2. Mathematics, including arithmetic, algebra, to include the solution of equations of the first degree containing one unknown quantity, the use of logarithms, the elements of plane geometry, plane trigonometry, and surveying.

3. Geography, particularly in reference to the United States and North America.

4. The outlines of general history, and particularly the history of the United States.

5. The Constitution of the United States and the organization of the Government under it, and the elements of international law.

6. Army regulations and the drill regulations of the arm from which the candidate is selected. The examination in drill regulations will be practical, extending through the school of the soldier, squad, and platoon, and shall take place on the parade-ground in the presence of the board.

7. The military records of the candidates as certified to by their company, post, and regimental commanders.

8. Physical aptitude, as determined by the med-

ical examination; proficiency in athletics, skill in field sports, etc.

9. Moral character and civil record as verified after a thorough investigation by the board.

In awarding marks the board will give to each subject in the examination the relative weight given in the form following below. The general average of the candidate will be computed as follows: Mark each question according to its relative weight, and reduce the aggregate of marks thus obtained in each subject to a scale of 100. The result will give the average of proficiency in the subject. Multiply the average in each subject by the number indicating

Example.

No.	Subject.	Average.	Relative weights.	Products of multiplication by relative weights.
1	English grammar, etc............	82	3	246
2	Mathematics.....................	76	4	304
3	Geography......................	80	2	160
4	History.........................	73	3	219
5	Constitutional and international law.	67	2	134
6	Army and drill regulations, etc.....	75	3	225
7	Military record..................	80	2	160
8	Physique.......................	75	3	225
9	Moral character and antecedents....	85	3	255
			25	1,928
				77·12

the relative weight of the subject, and divide the sum of the products by the sum of the relative weights; the quotient will be the general average. No candidate will be passed by the board who shall not have attained an average of 65 per cent in each subject of examination and a general average of at least 70 per cent.

V. When the board shall have examined and passed upon all the applicants, it will prepare a tabulated statement showing the order of their relative merit as developed by the examination, and forward the proceedings, with all papers pertaining thereto, to the adjutant-general.

Soldiers who successfully pass the final examination, and receive certificates as required by law, will be known in the service as "candidates for promotion," and will have the title of "candidate" prefixed to that of their rank on all rolls, returns, orders, and correspondence. They will be entitled to this privilege so long only as they maintain the specially honorable position of "candidate."

The right to appointment of a "candidate" who does not receive an appointment as second lieutenant in the meantime will expire on the first of September following his examination, unless he elects to appear before the board at Fort Leavenworth a second time for examination in competition with those who may be examined at the time of his second appearance. An applicant for re-examination will not be required to pass a departmental board a second time. In order to secure a re-examination, he will forward an application therefor through his regular military commanders (whose remarks will be indorsed thereon) to the adjutant-general, at least three months in advance of the time of holding the annual competitive examination. After re-examination he will take his place in the relative merit list with those examined at the time of his re-examination.

Applicants who fail to pass the competitive board at their first examination may secure a second examination in the same manner as candidates who pass and fail to receive an appointment.

No soldier will be re-examined who will pass the age limit prior to the date set for such re-examination.

"Candidates" who may be guilty of misconduct will be promptly reported to the adjutant-general of the army, through regimental and department headquarters, the report to give a full statement of the misconduct alleged, with names of witnesses. Before forwarding such report to the adjutant-general of the army, the department commander will see that the "candidate" has a fair and impartial hearing, that the merits of the case may be carefully and accurately determined and reported on for the decision of the Secretary of War.

"Candidates" will not be deprived of the privileges of their position except by sentence of court-martial as required by the law, or by the decision of the Secretary of War.

By command of Major-General Schofield:

R. WILLIAMS,
Adjutant-General.

METHOD OF MAKING APPLICATION.

By reference to paragraph I of the foregoing order, eligibility for promotion, so far as the right to making an application is concerned, is clearly outlined. If eligible, application for promotion should be made to the department commander in proper form on or before the 1st of February, accompanied by the information required in the following form:

Form for Individual Record of Candidate.

1. Give the exact date and place of your birth.
2. Are you married, or single?

3. Are you a citizen of the United States? If so, state whether native-born or naturalized.

4. What schools have you attended, and for what periods? Answer explicitly, giving dates, and designations of schools, as public schools, academies, district schools, colleges, manual-training schools, night schools, etc.

5. Have you ever been apprenticed to a trade? If so, to what trade, for what length of time?

6. In what occupation or trade have you been employed? Answer explicitly, giving time, character of employment, etc.

7. During what time have you supported yourself, totally or partially, by your own labor?

8. Have you ever served in the National Guard? Answer explicitly, giving State, arm of service, rank, etc.

(Signature) ....

Sworn to and subscribed before me, the...... day of.......... A. D. 189 .

Method of Selection.

Any unmarried soldier who is eligible under the law as to nationality, age, and character, may enter the competitive examination for promotion to the grade of second lieutenant in the army. A private has as much right to compete as a noncommissioned officer. The applicant may belong to any arm of the service or to any staff corps, for the law states very clearly that the competition shall be open to all *enlisted men of the army*. There is, therefore, no limit to the number who may compete, provided the above provisions of the law are fulfilled.

Character of Examinations.

The character and extent of the examinations are so clearly stated in the order just quoted that little remains to be said on these subjects. To give the applicant a more tangible idea of the extent and character of these examinations, a list of the questions propounded at a final examination at Fort Leavenworth is given at the close of this chapter.

Examinations are usually conducted on each subject in the order named. The time allowed to complete an examination on any subject may or may not be limited, but it usually takes about two weeks to complete the mental examination.

Applicants should bear in mind that different questions are asked each year; the ones given in this chapter are intended merely as a guide to what may be anticipated in future examinations.

It will be observed that the extent and character

of preliminary examination are the same as the character and extent of the final examination, but applicants who fail to pass the preliminary board will not be ordered for final competitive examination at Fort Leavenworth.

HINTS TO COMPETITORS.

Any soldier ambitious to rise to the grade of a commissioned officer will do wisely to examine closely all the requirements of the position he seeks, and the extent of the examinations he will have to pass to secure the prize. Being satisfied that he is physically, mentally, and morally equal to the occasion, he should make his application as previously described. As a rule, officers will do all in their power to assist a worthy man, although they may dislike to lose an efficient and valuable man. As to length of service, the regulations simply require that the candidate shall have served *at least two years* in the army. The service of a cadet honorably discharged from the United States Military Academy counts as "service in the army," and hence could be used to fulfill the conditions as regards length of service.

Applicants are referred to the "Points," in regard to the entrance examinations at the Military

Academy, which are given in the previous chapter, and most of which apply in the examination of competitors for promotion. If extra time is wanted in preparing for an examination, make a formal application for it to the post commander through your company commander, stating your reasons. A very good and proper rule which a company commander may follow is, never to recommend a man for promotion unless he feels that he would be glad to have the man as a second lieutenant of his own company.

Candidates for promotion should always behave in a soldierly manner, being prompt and cheerful in the obedience of all orders, remembering that one must first learn to obey before he can successfully command. The bearing and conduct of a candidate during examination are always taken into consideration by the board in determining his character and aptitude for the position he seeks. In the past ten years about one hundred noncommissioned officers have been promoted to the grade of second lieutenant in the army. There is no limit to the number that may be promoted from any one regiment, or even from any one company, but it has seldom happened that more than two have qualified from the same regiment in a single year.

As any soldier may now compete for promotion,

it is probable that there will be an increase in the number promoted from the army, for more young men may now be induced to enlist for that purpose. The increase, however, will necessarily be slight, for it seldom happens that there are more than a dozen vacancies in the army after the assignment of the class graduating from the Military Academy.

Assignment to Regiment.

The army regulations state that, as a rule, soldiers promoted to the grade of second lieutenant will be assigned to vacancies existing in the regiments from which they are promoted; but this is really more the exception than the rule, as the required vacancies do not always exist. But this is a matter of little importance, as there is now no particular advantage to be gained by being assigned to any particular regiment.

If vacancies exist in the army, candidates usually remain at Fort Leavenworth after completing the final examination until receipt of their appointments as second lieutenants.

The expenses of candidates from the army, going to and returning from examinations, are of course defrayed by the Government, and they receive pay, rations, etc., during examination, as they are considered quite as much on duty as if they were at their proper station. Successful candidates receive pay as officers from the day the new office is accepted. With the appointment comes the letter of assignment and the order directing each officer to join his new station on or before such a date, a delay of about thirty days being allowed to enable him to procure his uniform and equipments. Being under orders, his necessary traveling expenses will be paid by the Government. Many of the remarks under this head, near the close of Chapters I and III, are applicable in the case of officers promoted from the army, and their attention is invited to them.

Enlisting for a Commission.

The attention of those young men in civil life who may contemplate enlisting in the regular army with a view to obtaining a commission is invited to all that has been said in the present chapter concerning the promotion of meritorious soldiers. From this will be obtained all necessary information regarding the qualifications of such candidates, and this is the only path that will lead from the ranks to a commission.

The young man who is debating whether to

make the effort or not may wish to know, to begin with, what steps he must take in order to enter the army, and about what his duties may be as a soldier.

This information can easily be obtained by simply calling at any army recruiting office. These offices are located in all the principal cities of the United States, a list of which, with their location, is given in the Appendix. The same information may be had by calling at the adjutant's office at any military post in the United States which is garrisoned by troops belonging to the regular army. In short, any unmarried man between sixteen and thirty years of age, who is *physically sound*, of good moral character, and able to read and write the English language, can enlist in the regular army by applying to any of the recruiting offices referred to, or to the recruiting officer at any military post.

He must be at least five feet four inches in height, and weigh at least one hundred and twenty-eight pounds, and, if a minor, must have the consent of his parents or guardians. As the law requires a man to serve at least two years in the army before he is eligible for *final* examination for promotion, and as no man over thirty years of age will be commissioned, a young man enlisting with a view to obtaining a commission should not be over twenty-seven years old. Although these seem to be very simple conditions for the ordinary man to fulfill, it may be interesting to know that at present only about one man in five who presents himself for enlistment succeeds in passing the examination. Some are rejected on general appearance, others for not being able to show evidence of good character, and the rest for failure to pass physically.

Strange as it may seem to some, the regular army is not composed of a set of loafers and tramps, or rascals who wish to escape the penalties of the civil law. True, a few of these vagabonds find their way into the army; but if you select twenty-five thousand lawyers, doctors, or twenty-five thousand men of any one profession in the United States, among that number a sprinkling of black sheep will be found. The majority of the enlisted men of the army are obedient, industrious, and honest, and are deserving of more credit for their intelligence and soldierly conduct than is ever given to them by the average American citizen. That menial or degrading services are required of soldiers is sheer nonsense.

It is true that they make their own beds and

fires, cook their own food, and dust their own clothes, and are required to keep their quarters neat and clean; but this much is required of cadets at the Military Academy, and it is not considered to be beneath their station or calling. An officer or soldier who can not care for himself in time of peace, is liable to starve or die from ignorant exposure in time of war.

This short dissertation is given simply to insure the young man desirous of enlisting for a commission that he will not be casting his lot among the toughest element in the land, which is quite a popular belief regarding the army. He will find men in nearly every company of the army who are his equal in many respects, and his superior in others. It is not intended by the foregoing to induce young men of good breeding and superior intellectual attainments to enter the army with a view to obtaining a commission; for the enlisting of such a man is a serious question, as he may be unable to succeed in his efforts, and be sorry for the step he has taken.

The young man who is sufficiently well educated to pass his examinations for a commission may be totally unfit and unable to undergo the discipline and duty required of the average soldier in the ranks. Life might be so unbearable that he would not serve another month if he could get out of it. But that young man is equally unfit to become a commissioned officer; for a man unable to perform the duties of the ordinary soldier for two or three years, would be useless as an officer. Hence, he has missed his calling, and never should have enlisted. The young man who enlists for a commission must not only be physically, morally, and intellectually capable of passing the required examinations, but he needs, above all, good common sense combined with what is known as backbone or grit, and sufficient tact to accommodate himself to circumstances. In general, he will be comfortably housed, well fed and well clothed, and will receive sufficient pay to defray all necessary expenses. Socially, he may not have the advantages to which he has been accustomed, but amusements of various kinds are got up and enjoyed by every garrison. Schools for his education, libraries, and reading-rooms containing valuable books and leading periodicals of the day, are maintained at every post in the army. Many of the companies and some of the posts have gymnasiums, and pool and billiard rooms, which afford amusement and exercise. All of these, except the pool and billiard rooms, are kept up by the Government, and billiards and pool never cost more than five cents a game. For purposes of discipline there is more or less of a gulf between the men and their officers, which is particularly true of their social life. Right here is where his *grit* and *tact* come in play; for, no matter what his previous station in life may have been, it would not become him to presume to throw himself forward or above his comrades, no matter how much he or his friends might desire it. He must come into the service prepared to take what falls to his lot, doing his duty without complaint, for it is only "old soldiers" who claim the right to "growl." Remember, you are a soldier, and must do a soldier's duty to entitle you to the respect and confidence of your comrades. Show due respect at all times to your superiors, be manly and impartial to your inferiors, prompt and cheerful in the obedience of all lawful orders.

Selection of Arm of Service.

Shall I enlist in the infantry, cavalry, or artillery? will be the question that a young man from civil life desiring promotion will ask. In time of peace artillery enjoys good stations, but the men have to learn infantry as well as artillery drill. Cavalry have the worst stations, and the men have horses to care for, besides arms and equipments *galore*.

The infantry have good stations, and the men have less to do, and less to learn in time of peace, than either of the other arms. In time of war, as General Sherman has said, "infantry is the backbone of the army." But it is believed that any officer, after a moment's thought, would advise his friend desiring to obtain a commission in the easiest manner and in the shortest period of time, to join the infantry first, the artillery next, the cavalry last.

Pay and Discharges.

According to recent laws, a man in the first enlistment may now be discharged from the army after three years' honorable service by simply requesting it. Or, after one year's service, he can purchase his discharge by paying to the United States five dollars for every month he has yet to serve to complete three years' service. For example, should a man desire to leave the service at the end of one year, by paying to the Government the sum of one hundred and twenty dollars he will receive his discharge.

So it is now an easy matter to get out of the army if one finds he does not like it. The pay of a man for the first two years of his service is thirteen dollars per month, besides good quarters, clothes, and food, and plenty of them. Each year after the second the pay increases one dollar per month, and, of course, noncommissioned officers receive an increase of a few dollars per month over the private. The average pay of staff sergeants is about forty dollars per month.

Final Examination Questions, Fort Leavenworth.

Grammar.

1. Give the parts of speech, with the modifications to which each is subject.

2. Define each modification.

3. When is each case used, and how is each formed, in both simple and compound words?

4. What are the relative pronouns, and when is each used?

5. Into what general classes are adjectives divided? Give an example of each.

6. How are verbs divided with respect to meaning? Define each, and give examples.

7. Define the different voices of verbs, and give examples of a verb in each voice.

8. Define the different moods of verbs, and give examples of a verb in each.

9. How are participles used? Give examples.

10. How are adverbs classified with reference to meaning? Give examples of each.

11. What is the office of the preposition?

12. How are conjunctions classified? Give examples.

13. Correct the following sentences (giving reasons):

(1) This is a man whom I think deserves encouragement.

(2) The Senate of the United States are a more dignified body than the House of Representatives.

(3) The court is unable to agree.

(4) This is one of the most valuable books that has appeared in any language.

(5) The condition of the crops show that the country has suffered much.

(6) To read and write were once an honorary distinction.

(7) The public is often deceived by false appearances.

(8) Charles formed expensive habits and by those means became poor.

(9) It is difficult in some cases to distinguish between an interrogatory and exclamatory sentence.

(10) There is no doubt of the bill passing the house.

(11) The dress was made by Worth, the milliner, he that we saw in Paris.

(12) My father allowed my brother and I to accompany him.

(13) I would act the same part if I were him.

(14) They seemed to be nearly dressed alike.

(15) At home I studied geometry, that I found useful afterwards.

(16) Who did you vote for?

(17) The money is to be divided between the three brothers.

(18) As far as I am able to judge the book is well written.

(19) Either you or I are in the way.

(20) An account of the great events in all parts of the world are given in the daily papers.

14. Analyze and parse the following sentence: "To enable them to prepare for examination, candidates will, when practicable, be designated to appear six months in advance."

Spelling.

Cellule.	Synchronous.
Mignonette.	Hæmorrhage.
Recommend.	Syzygy.
Awry.	Femoral.

Presbytery. Sibylline.
Salable. Pellucid.
Myrrh. Pyrites.
Diphthong. Hydropathy.
Chemise. Palladium.
Vedette. Coliseum.
Purloin. Panegyric.
Petard. Empyrean.

Dictation.

While the *doughty* king was engaged in war the *roguish dauphin* spent his time in the pleasure of his own *coterie*. His raillery and *innuendoes* occasionally stirred his companions from their sycophancy into something like a display of manly independence; but this, reacting on the changeable nature of their *liege* lord, ruffled his complaisance, and they relapsed into their former state.

Define the words in italics in the foregoing.

Arithmetic.

1. What is the least number of cents that will pay for a number of peaches at $3/4$ of a cent each, a number of apples at $2/3$ of a cent each, and a number of pears at $5/6$ of a cent each?

2. Find the difference between seven thousand

and seven thousandths, and divide the remainder by seven millionths.

3. If by selling a horse at $80 I lose $12\frac{1}{2}$ per cent of the first cost, shall I gain or lose, and what per cent by selling him at $90?

4. What per cent of 455 is 10·25?

5. Add seventy-five hundredths, eight and sixty-seven thousandths, seven and three hundred and fifty-four thousandths.

6. Divide two hundred and twenty-two ten thousandths by one and twenty-five hundredths, and reduce result to a common fraction in its lowest terms.

7. Reduce $\dfrac{9^{19}/_{21}}{1/_{5}}$ and $\dfrac{9/_{26}}{1/_{3}}$ to decimal fractions and multiply one by the other.

8. How much of each kind of tea, worth 72, 54, and 48 cents, will be required to make a mixture of 100 pounds worth 60 cents per pound?

9. If 320,000 bricks 9 in. long, 5 in. broad, and $2\frac{1}{4}$ in. thick are required for the construction of a building, how many bricks 12 in. long, 6 in. broad, and 3 in. thick would be required for the same purpose?

10. If $\frac{4}{5}$ of a bushel of oats be required for $\frac{2}{3}$ of a bushel of corn, what is the cost of a bushel of oats when corn is $\frac{3}{4}$ of a dollar a bushel?

11. What part of $13/25 + 8/21$ is $7\tfrac{1}{7} - 4/5$?

12. A man travels 3 miles the first day, 5 the second, 7 the third, and so on, till he went 57 miles in one day, how many days had he traveled at the close of the last day?

Logarithms.

1. $4{\cdot}95 \times 6981{\cdot}7 \times 56 \times {\cdot}009872$.
2. $\dfrac{58472}{89{\cdot}54}$.
3. $\dfrac{876543 \times {\cdot}03542}{{\cdot}7654 \times 321{\cdot}28}$.
4. $(15)^5$.
5. $({\cdot}00009)^{-2/3}$.
6. $(2364)^{3/4}$.
7. $\sqrt[3]{(1/00006)^2}$.
8. Side $A = \dfrac{\sin 25° \ 10' \ 15'' \times 198}{\sin 125° \ 54' \ 10''}$.
9. $\cos \tfrac{1}{2} A = \sqrt{\dfrac{\sin (105° \ 24' \ 7'') \sin (31° \ 1' \ 8'')}{\sin (35° \ 45' \ 14'') \sin (100° \ 39')}}$.
10. $\tan \tfrac{1}{2}(A+B) = \dfrac{\cos(26°12'20'') \cot(75°12'6'')}{\cos(36° \ 25' \ 39'')}$.

Algebra.

1. Multiply $x + 1/2 \bullet x^2 - 1/4 \bullet^2 x^3$ by $1 - 1/2 \bullet x + 1/4 \bullet^2 x^2$.

2. Divide $15x^3y^3 + 15y^5 + 10x^2y^5 + 6x^6 + 6x^3y^2 - 5x^5y^2 - 9x^2y^4 - 6x^4y^4$ by $2x^2y^2 + 3x^3 + 3y^2$.

3. Divide $8 + 12x^{-1} + 2x^{-2} + 2x^{-4}$ by $x^{-2} - 2x^{-1} + 4$, and write result with positive exponents.

4. Find the G. C. D. of $20x^6 - 12x^5 + 16x^4 - 15x^3 + 14x^2 - 15x + 4$ and $15x^4 - 9x^3 + 47x^2 - 21x + 28$.

5. Find the L. C. multiple of $x^4 - 10x^2 + 9x^4 + 10x^3 + 20x^2 - 10x - 21$, and $x^4 + 4x^3 - 22x^2 - 4x + 21$.

6. $\dfrac{x(a+x)}{a-x} + \dfrac{5ax-x^2}{x-2} + \dfrac{2a^2}{a-x}$.

7. $\left(\dfrac{x^2}{a^2} - \dfrac{x}{a} + 1\right)\left(\dfrac{x^2}{a^2} + \dfrac{x}{a} + 1\right)$.

8. $\dfrac{x^4 - b^4}{x^2 - 2bx + b^2} \div \dfrac{x^2 + bx}{x - b}$.

9. Find the value of x in the following equation:
$$\left(x + \dfrac{a}{2}\right)\left(x - \dfrac{b}{2}\right) - \left(x+b\right)\left(x-a\right) + \dfrac{b}{4} = 0.$$

10. Find the value of x in the following:
$$4\cdot 8x - \dfrac{\cdot 72x - \cdot 05}{\cdot 5} = 1\cdot 6x + 8\cdot 9.$$

Geometry.

1. In equal triangles what parts must be equal—or, how many parts of equal triangles must be equal, and what are they?

2. What is the sum of the angles of any triangle equal to? Demonstrate it.

3. What is the sum of the exterior angles of any polygon equal to? Demonstrate it.

4. How many circumferences may be made to pass through any three points not in the same straight line? Demonstrate it.

5. In equal circles what is the relation between angles at the center and the intercepted arcs? Demonstrate it.

6. What is the measure of an angle inscribed in a circle? Demonstrate it.

7. In any triangle, what is the square of the side opposite an acute angle equal to? opposite an obtuse angle? Demonstrate it.

8. How does a line drawn parallel to the base of a triangle divide the other two sides? Demonstrate.

9. When are triangles similar?

10. What is the relation between the perimeters of similar polygons and also between their areas?

Trigonometry.

1. How is a plane angle measured?
2. What is meant by the complement of an arc?
3. What is meant by the supplement of an arc?
4. What parts of a triangle must be known in order that the other parts may be determined?
5. Draw a diagram showing the different functions of the arc used in trigonometry.
6. What is meant by the natural sine, cosine, etc.?
7. Given, two angles, $A = 30° \ 25' \ 40''$, $C = 95° \ 18' \ 10''$, and side $AC = 40$; determine the other sides.
8. Given, two sides, $CB = 80.75$, $AC = 68.05$, and the included angle $= 125° \ 48' \ 10''$; determine the other side.
9. Given, the sides of a triangle, 288,500, and 384; determine the angles.
10. The base of a right-angled triangle is 384, the perpendicular 288; determine the other parts.

Elements of Surveying.

1. In the measurement of distances with the chain alone, how is a line prolonged beyond an obstacle, when it can not be seen over?
2. Using the surveyor's compass, how are correc-

tions made for local attractions, and how are the field-notes kept?

3. Required, the contents and plot of a piece of land of which the following are the field-notes:

STATIONS.	BEARINGS.	DISTANCES.
1	N 52 E	10·64
2	S 29¾ E	4·09
3	S 31¾ W	7·68
4	N 61 W	7·24

4. Describe the method of finding the true meridian with the compass.

5. Describe the vernier, and the manner of reading an instrument by it.

6. How are horizontal angles measured with the transit?

7. How are distances measured, using the stadia, or micrometer, and rod?

8. Given in outline the principles upon which a trigonometrical survey of a section of country is made.

9. Describe the manner of locating the positions of any three points in a survey by means of a plane table.

10. Explain the manner of finding the differ-

ence of level between two points with the Y-level. Show the manner of keeping the field-notes.

Geography.

1. What countries lie entirely within the Eastern hemisphere? What countries lie entirely within the Western hemisphere? What countries lie partly within both hemispheres?

2. Define latitude and longitude, and show how the latter corresponds to time, and why.

3. On what general principles are maps constructed? Explain the uses of scales on maps.

4. What is a mountain system? Give an example of one in North America, in South America, in Asia, and in Africa.

5. What is a river system? Give an example of one in each of the foregoing countries.

6. Give the positions of the following countries on the globe; name the waters by which their coasts are washed, their principal exports, and the names of the races of people occupying them: British America; the United States, including Alaska; Mexico; Central America; France; Denmark; Russia; India; Arabia; Australia; Japan; and South America.

7. Name the five largest rivers, giving their

sources, lengths, and mouths, in North America; the three highest mountains; the three largest lakes, with their outlets. Which is the highest mountain in the United States east of the Mississippi River?

8. Name the three largest rivers in South America, giving their sources, lengths, and mouths; the highest mountain-peak in South America.

9. Name the provinces constituting the Dominion of Canada. What is the form of government of the Dominion?

10. What are the principal islands in the Caribbean Sea? What is the name of the first island discovered by Columbus? To what group of islands does it belong?

11. Where does the Gulf Stream originate? In what direction does it flow, and what effect has it on the climate of the countries near which it passes? What produces it? What stream on the Pacific coast resembles it in origin and effects?

12. What are the chief agricultural products of the United States on the Atlantic coast—in the Mississippi River basin? Why is the climate of the Pacific coast so different from that of the Atlantic coast?

13. Where are the outlets of the Humboldt and

Carson Rivers? Into what does the Saskatchewan flow?

14. Where is the Congo Free State? Bound it.

15. Where are the divides, or water-sheds, separating the sources of the following rivers?—The Missouri from the Columbia; the Ohio from the Hudson; the Rhine from the Danube; the Congo from the Nile.

16. Where is the Argentine Republic situated? Name its three principal cities. How far does Chili extend along the coast of South America? To what country does the Isthmus of Panama belong?

17. Name some of the chief productions of Mexico. What railroads connect Mexico with the United States? What is the principal harbor on the eastern coast? on the western coast?

18. Where is St. George's Channel? the Irish Sea? Name the four principal rivers in France. Where are the Vosges Mountains? Where is Vladivostocks? Where is the Punjaub, and what river flows through it? What country borders on the west?

19. Where is Copenhagen? To what government does Hong-Kong belong? What kingdoms are comprised in the German Empire? Where is Iceland situated, and to what government does it

belong? About opposite what State of the United States is Bermuda situated?

20. What is the shortest *fresh-water* route from Chicago to New York? to Philadelphia? By what route can a letter be sent in the shortest time from London to Yokohama? A ship sailing from Norfolk, Va., to Melbourne, without going through the Suez Canal, would take what route? What route would be traveled by a ship sailing from Liverpool to Canton *via* Suez Canal? The Suez Canal being closed, what route would a ship sailing from Cronstadt to Vladivostock have to take? In going from Burlington, Vt., to Vicksburg, Miss., in a straight line, what States would you pass through?

History.

1. Give a brief account of the military exploits of Alexander the Great.

2. Give a brief summary of the military operations of Hannibal.

3. Give a brief summary of the military exploits of Julius Cæsar.

4. Who were the Huns, Goths, and Vandals? Where did they come from? And who were the principal leaders of each engaged at different times in attacking Rome and overrunning her territory?

5. Give a short account of Charlemagne's career, and state the greatest extent of country ruled over by him.

6. State briefly the origin of the Crusades, and the most important results.

7. When did the fall of Constantinople, and the consequent fall of the Eastern Empire, take place?

8. Who were the rulers of France, Spain, and England when the Reformation began?

9. What were the most important results of the defeat of the Spanish armada?

10. Give a brief summary of the career of Oliver Cromwell. What was the English Commonwealth, and how long did it last?

11. What was the Revolution of 1688 in England, and how brought about? Name some of the provisions of the Bill of Rights.

12. When did the Seven Years' War begin and end? Name three battles in which Frederick was victorious, and two in which he lost.

13. When was Napoleon first crowned Emperor of France? Give a brief summary of his military operations in 1805. What great naval battle was fought in that year?

14. Give a summary of the causes, direct and in-

direct, which brought about the American Revolution, 1776.

15. Give a brief account of the battle of Long Island, and the subsequent operations of the American troops up to and including the battle of Trenton. What were the immediate effects of the victory gained by Washington?

16. What were the most important results to the Americans of Burgoyne's surrender?

17. When were the Articles of Confederation adopted by the thirteen States? What title did the confederacy take under these articles? What powers were granted to the General Government?

18. Give a brief account of the military operations which led to the surrender of Cornwallis's army? Where and when was the treaty of peace between the United States and England signed?

19. What were the causes of Shays's rebellion?

20. When was the Federal Constitution adopted, and when did the first Congress authorized by it assemble? What name was given to the members of the party supporting the Constitution? to the one opposing it? When were the names of Republican and Democratic first given to political parties in the United States?

21. Give a brief account of the causes of the

Whisky Insurrection. When did it occur, and how was it suppressed?

22. Give the boundaries of the territory added to the United States by the Louisiana purchase of 1803.

23. When, without any actual declaration of war, did hostilities begin between the United States and France? Name some of the vessels engaged in action. What claims were made against the United States by some of their citizens, growing out of this state of affairs?

24. Name some of the causes, direct and indirect, which led to the declaration of war against England in 1812.

25. What was the Missouri Compromise? When adopted? When repealed?

26. Give a brief account of the nullification acts of South Carolina in 1832. What resulted from them?

27. State briefly the causes of the war between the United States and Mexico. What were the terms of the treaty made between the two powers at the close of the war? What is the Gadsden purchase?

28. Give a brief account of the battles of Gettysburg and Nashville, the names of the generals com-

manding on both sides, the results of the battles, etc.

29. What were the Alabama claims, and how disposed of?

30. When did the United States resume specie payment after the war of the rebellion, 1861–'65?

Constitutional Law.

1. Into how many departments does the Constitution distribute the powers of the Government of the United States? Explain the powers of each, and how they deal as regards time.

2. The Constitution, in enumerating the powers which shall be exercised by authority of the General Government, confers them in terms upon Congress. What are they?

(1) Finances, (2) commerce, (3) commercial, (4) penalties, (5) postal, (6) patent and copyrights, (7) war, (8) judiciary, (9) naturalization, (10) territory, (11) states, (12) executive vacancy, (13) appointments, (14) constitutional amendments, (15) slavery, (16) general law-making, (17) meeting.

3. Enumerate the prohibitions on the United States.

(1) *Habeas corpus*, (2) direct taxes, (3) export

duties, (4) interstate commerce, (5) public money, (6) nobility, (7) penalties, (8) foreign slave trade, (9) repudiation, (10) freedom.

4. Enumerate the prohibitions on the States.

(1) State relations, (2) commerce, (3) war, (4) penalties, (5) nobility, (6) duties, (7) slavery.

5. What rights are reserved to the States?

(1) Representation, (2) citizenship, (3) state amity, (4) new States, (5) elections, (6) militia officers, (7) Federal protection, (8) fugitives, (9) reservations.

6. What personal rights are guaranteed under the Constitution?

(1) Domicile, (2) security, (3) judicial, (4) criminal actions, (5) civil actions, (6) treason, (7) official immunities.

7. Where is the judicial power of the Government vested?

8. Jurisdiction of the judicial power?

9. In what cases has the Supreme Court original jurisdiction?

10. In what cases appellate jurisdiction?

11. Define citizenship.

12. By what process may an alien be made a citizen? Explain the steps required, and give exceptions in favor of soldiers.

13. Give the three processes by which a bill may become a law.

14. What are *ex post facto* laws?

15. In what case has the President no pardoning power?

16. How are treaties made?

17. What two methods of proposing and ratifying amendments to the Constitution?

18. In what does treason consist, and what is necessary to convict?

19. Explain the difference between taxes, duties, imposts, and excises.

20. In case of the removal, death, resignation, or inability of both the President and Vice-President, give the order of presidential succession.

International Law.

1. Who are parties to international law?

2. What do you understand by the sovereignty of a State?

3. How are governments classified? Name and define each.

4. How are sovereign powers classified?

5. How is the national character of an individual determined?

6. Define extradition, and by what three ways it may be effected.

7. As nations can not treat directly with each other, how is intercourse between them carried on, and how classified?

8. For what purposes are consuls appointed?

9. Define treaties, their purpose. To whom does the right of making treaties belong?

10. In case of conflict of international rights, what three ways of adjusting these differences are most frequently resorted to?

11. Without resorting to war, what two means of redress involving the use of forcible or hostile measures are there?

12. Define combatant and noncombatant, and state under which class you would place surgeons and chaplains.

13. In case of war, what methods of communication between belligerents in the field?

14. What is the distinction between safe-conduct and safeguards?

15. What is a spy?

16. What is the distinction between guerrillas and partisans?

17. What do you understand by contraband of war?

18. Define blockade.

19. What constitutes a valid blockade?

20. What do you understand by the belligerent right of search?

Army Regulations.

1. The post noncommissioned staff shall consist of—?

2. Where is the military control of noncommissioned officers of the general staff serving at posts not occupied by troops vested?

3. What will enlisted men detached from their companies be provided with, and what must it show?

4. In what ways may an enlisted man be discharged before the expiration of service?

5. What books of record will be kept at each post?

6. How are sergeants and corporals appointed?

7. How first sergeants?

8. Who are artificers?

9. Name the company books of record. Describe their use, and how kept.

10. When is a board of survey necessary for unserviceable stores?

11. By whom is property condemned?

12. How many kinds of orders are there? How numbered and denominated?

Practical Examination in Infantry Drill Regulations.

Immediately preceding the execution of each movement, candidates will give the proper commands and explanations of it. Also correct any errors occurring in their subdivisions during the execution of movements.

School of the Soldier and Squad.

Facings.—Right; left; rear.

Setting up Exercise.—One each of arm; trunk; leg.

Steps.—Side; change step.

Manual of Arms.—Being at the order, all of it by the numbers, including loadings and firings—standing, kneeling, and lying. Align the squad.

Bayonet Exercise.—Take distance to the front and go through the whole exercise.

Extended Order.—Deploy to the front; on the line; extend and close intervals; rally; assemble.

School of Platoon.—As chiefs of platoons, all

movements by platoons in the school of the company.

Extended Order.—Deploy the whole platoon to the front into line of squads; assemble on right squad, first section; from a halt, deploy first section into line of skirmishers, holding second section as reserve; extend and close intervals on right squad; assemble on left squad, first section; form column of fours; form right front into line of squads; deploy as skirmishers; rally by sections; assemble on first section; form column of fours; form on right into line of squads; take one section as reserve and re-enforce the firing-line according to the different methods, using the approximate fire for each case, and giving instructions in the natural cover.

Practical Examination in Cavalry Drill Regulations.

Immediately preceding the execution of each movement, candidates will give the proper commands and explanations of it. Also correct any errors occurring in their subdivisions during the execution of movements.

School of the Soldier and Squad.

Facings.—Right; left; rear.

Setting up Exercise.—One each of arm; trunk; leg.

Steps.—Side; change step.

Manual of Arms.—Being at the order, execute by numbers, right shoulder; carry; port; carry; sling carbines; unsling carbines; loadings and firings; standing, kneeling, and lying.

Extended Order Dismounted.—Deploy as skirmishers to front; assemble by squads; deploy to right flank; form line of squads to the right front from column of fours; assemble.

Trooper Mounted.—Dismount and mount (horse saddled); draw saber; execute right, left, and rear moulinets; raise, charge saber; right, left, and rear cuts; right, left, and rear points; right, left, right and left low parries; head parry, against infantry right parry; same, left parry.

School of Platoon.—As chiefs, four designated movements.

Extended Order Mounted.—Form line of squads, from halt and marching. Deploy on interior squad, halt platoon, form column of fours, form line of squads to right, front, and halt; to the right, and halt. Form line of squads, deploy to right front, left front, to a flank.

Platoon deployed, rally it; assemble it; rally by squads; to fight on foot; action left front; right front; left. Assemble platoon dismounted, deploy into line of squads, keeping one as support. Then into skirmishers, and execute the different firings by squads, rapid fire, etc., used in making an attack.

CHAPTER III.

COMMISSIONS FROM CIVIL LIFE.

As previously stated, the law provides that appointments to the grade of second lieutenant in the army are given first to the graduates of the Military Academy, and, should any vacancies yet exist, then to certain meritorious soldiers of the army, and, last, to such persons from civil life as the President of the United States may elect. "Appointments of civilians, except of graduates of the Military Academy who have been honorably discharged, will not be made in time of peace, unless more vacancies exist than will be required in the assignment of the next graduating class." Therefore the selection of civilians for these positions rests solely with the President, and he has prescribed certain conditions which must be fulfilled prior to issuing these appointments, which are outlined in the following order from the War Department:

HEADQUARTERS OF THE ARMY,
ADJUTANT GENERAL'S OFFICE,
Washington, August 10, 1891.

GENERAL ORDERS, No. 72.

By direction of the Secretary of War, the following rules governing the examination of candidates for the appointment of second lieutenant in the army of the United States from civil life are substituted for those prescribed in General Orders, No. 5, of 1890, from this office, and are published for the information and government of all concerned. The educational conditions herein prescribed are essential in connection with the schools for commissioned officers at Forts Leavenworth and Monroe:

I. No person shall be examined unless he has a letter from the War Department authorizing his examination.

If the candidate has been graduated at an institution where he received military instruction, he must present a recommendation from the faculty of the institution.

If a member of the National Guard, he must present recommendations from the proper National Guard authorities.

II. Every candidate will be subjected to a rigid physical examination, and if there be found to exist any cause of disqualification to such a degree as might in the future impair his efficiency as an officer of the army he will be rejected. The board will inquire and report concerning each applicant whether he is of good moral character or addicted to the use of intoxicating liquors. Examination as to physical qualifications shall conform to the standard required of recruits, and shall include a certificate of physical examination by two medical officers to accompany the proceedings of the board (which shall embrace all the information required by the form for the examination of recruits).

III. No candidate will be examined who is under twenty-one or over twenty-seven years of age; who, in the judgment of the board, is not physically qualified to discharge all the duties of an officer in active service; who has any deformity of body or mental infirmity, or whose moral habits are bad.

IV. The board, being satisfied as to these preliminary points, will proceed to examine each candidate separately:

1. In his knowledge of English grammar, and his ability to read, write, and spell with facility and correctness.

2. In his knowledge of arithmetic, and his ability to apply its rules to all practical questions; in

his knowledge of the use of logarithms and ability to apply them to questions of practice ; in his knowledge of algebra, to include the solution of simple equations ; and in his knowledge of geometry, plane trigonometry, and the elements of surveying.

3. In his knowledge of geography, particularly in reference to the northern continent of America.

4. In his knowledge of the outlines of general history, and particularly the history of his own country.

5. In his knowledge of the Constitution of the United States and the organization of the Government under it, and the elements of international law.

6. The board, having examined into the mental qualifications of each candidate and his character for sobriety and fidelity, shall also inquire into his general qualifications, aptitude, and probable efficiency as an officer of the army.

V. In awarding marks, the board will give to each subject in the examination the relative weight given in the form following below.

The general average of the candidate will be computed as follows:

Mark each question according to its relative weight, and reduce the aggregate of marks thus obtained in each subject to a scale of one hundred. The result will give the average of proficiency in the subject. Multiply the average in each subject by the number indicating the relative weight of the subject, and divide the sum of the products by the sum of the relative weights; the quotient will be the general average. No candidate will be passed by the board who shall not have attained an average of 65 per cent in each subject of examination, and a general average of at least 70 per cent.

Example.

No.	Subjects.	Averages.	Relative weights.	Products of multiplication by relative weights.
1	English grammar....................	82	3	246
2	Arithmetic, algebra, etc............	76	4	304
3	Geography.........................	80	2	160
4	History............................	73	3	219
5	Constitutional and international law.	65	2	130
6	Aptitude and probable efficiency....	95	3	285
			17	1.344
	General average................			79 1/17

VI. When an examining board shall have passed upon more than one candidate, the order of relative merit of all candidates examined by the board will be reported.

VII. Boards for the examination of applicants from civil life for appointment to commission in the army will be appointed by the Secretary of War, and shall consist of five commissioned officers, including two medical officers. The duties of the medical officers will be confined to inquiring into and reporting upon the physical qualifications of the candidates.

The proceedings of the board will be forwarded to the Adjutant-General.

By command of Major-General Schofield:

J. C. KELTON,
Adjutant General.

By comparing the foregoing order with the corresponding one giving the rules governing the examination for promotion of meritorious soldiers of the army to the grade of second lieutenant, it will be seen that, practically, the mental, moral, and physical examinations are the same. The only material difference is that noncommissioned officers are examined in drill and army regulations, and candidates from civil life are not examined in these subjects. The method of marking examination papers and the averages to be attained are the same. Therefore, in order not to make unnecessary repeti-

FROM CIVIL LIFE. 115

tions, the civilian candidate is referred to so much of the examinations of noncommissioned officers of the army as are applicable to his case. A list of the questions asked by an examining board in 1891 is, however, given for his information and guidance. Many of the "points" suggested to candidates appointed to the Military Academy relative to their entrance examination are also applicable in the examination of civilians for appointment to the grade of second lieutenant in the army, and their attention is invited to them. It will also be noted that competitors from the army are required to undergo two examinations, while but one is prescribed for the civilian candidate.

MANNER OF MAKING APPLICATION.

Applications are made usually to the Secretary of War or to the President of the United States. An application should be in writing, should state age, birthplace, residence, and qualifications of the applicant, accompanied by such recommendations of institutions of learning and prominent men as are obtainable.

Should vacancies in the army exist after the assignment of the graduating class at West Point, and of such meritorious soldiers as may have been duly recommended for promotion, the applications of civilian candidates are considered at the War Department. Successful applicants are then duly informed, and directed to appear before an army examining board, which is to determine their fitness for the position of second lieutenant in the army.

PLACE AND METHOD OF EXAMINATION.

In past years the examining boards have met at Washington, D. C., or Fort Monroe, Va., but they may meet at Fort Leavenworth, Kan., or any other suitable place. As civilians are at their own expense during examination it is customary to hold it at some central point, and where army officers are available. The examination takes place, as a rule, in the fall of the year.

The board meets, usually, about 10 A. M. The first day is given up to the physical examination of the candidates, which, as already explained, is very rigid. The candidates will then present such testimonials as to character as they may desire, having, previous to the physical examination, tendered their letter from the War Department authorizing them to appear before the board.

Boards sometimes require candidates to write a brief history of themselves from their fifteenth birthday. The mental examination is then begun, usually taking the subjects in their order.

In some cases the time for completing an examination is limited; in others it may not be. This rests with the board of examiners.

As soon as possible the examination papers are passed upon by the board, and its proceedings, which include its recommendations, together with the examination papers of each candidate, are forwarded to the adjutant-general of the army, who, at as early a date as practicable, will inform each candidate as to the result of the examination. The successful candidates will receive their appointments as second lieutenants in the army.

The examining board may or may not choose to inform the candidates as to the result of their examinations, but it is usually the part of prudence to remain silent on this point, as their recommendations may not be approved by the War Department, and hence false hopes will have been entertained by the candidates, which, to say the least, will not be pleasant.

HINTS TO CANDIDATES.

The difficulty of obtaining an appointment to the army from civil life may be estimated when it is known that where there is a vacancy for *one ap-*

pointment there are on file at the War Department at least *one hundred* applications for it.

Recently the sons of army officers, distinguished graduates of military schools, and promising young officers of the National Guard have received the majority of these appointments. From 1884 to 1890 only two or three such appointments were made, there being no vacancies in the army. In 1891 about twenty appointments were made from civil life, due to certain legislation which caused an unusual number of vacancies by the retirement of a large number of officers disabled as a result of wounds received or exposure during the rebellion. The probabilities of many such appointments being made each year in the near future are not promising.

It will be noted that the last clause of the rules for examination directs the examining board to "inquire into the candidate's general qualifications, aptitude, and probable efficiency as an officer of the army." On this subject the board awards a mark which counts as much in determining the general average as grammar or history. Hence attention should be directed to this subject. The points that will be considered in this respect are the extent of the instruction the candidate has received outside of his mere mental examination on the subjects enumerated. Being a graduate of a college, military training, or experience in army matters, or knowledge of other matters that affect an officer's efficiency, such as being more or less experienced in the control of men, are all subjects that would add weight to a candidate's examination.

In studying for examination there is but little choice in the selection of text-books, as any of the books used in modern schools treating of the required subjects will be sufficient authority. On constitutional and international law the following works are authority in the army, although many others will answer quite as well: Cooley's Constitutional Law and Davis's International Law. It might be well to state the name of the author of each text-book studied on the corresponding examination paper.

It is a popular belief that army officers have nothing to do in time of peace, and that their time is spent in ease and luxury. Some persons have the impression that the average army officer is always dancing and flirting. Others suppose he gambles and is intemperate in his habits.

If the reader is desirous of entering the army as an officer and is possessed of any of the foregoing opinions, and supposes that his fortune is made and all work ended when he succeeds in getting a commission, he will find that he is wonderfully mistaken, for idleness and intemperance are the exceptions, and not the rule.

Besides the usual routine garrison duties, such as guard, drill, parades, courts, boards, etc., every post in the army is a school. During the winter months theoretical instruction is imparted in the art and science of war, military topography, field engineering, etc., and each officer prepares and reads essays on military subjects. Besides this, he acts as instructor at the various schools for noncommissioned officers, where theoretical instruction is given in the drill regulations, manual of guard duty, and firing regulations. The summer months are spent in camp, on the rifle range, and putting in practice the theoretical knowledge obtained at school in winter.

Rigid theoretical and practical examinations have to be passed by every officer prior to promotion. Should he fail, he is given a year to prepare, during which time he loses his promotion. Should he fail at the second examination, he is dropped from the rolls of the army. The examination covers the art and science of war, military surveying and topography, field engineering, military and international law, and laws of war, army, drill, and firing regulations, and other service manuals.

Assignment to Regiment.

Officers appointed to the army from civil life may be assigned to any arm of the service, but the War Department appoints the great majority of them to the infantry and cavalry, and unless particular personal reasons exist no single regiment has any special advantages. The pay begins from the date of acceptance of appointment, but a person appointed from civil life is required to bear all expenses incurred until he has joined his first station, which is generally some large military post, not necessarily the station of his own regiment, where he remains for a few months to learn the preliminary duties of an officer.

If you wish, however, to be assigned to a particular regiment or arm of the service a letter to that effect should be addressed to the adjutant general of the army, at Washington, as soon as your examination is completed, stating your reasons for desiring such an assignment.

Many of the remarks near the close of Chapter I, on Assignment to Regiment, apply with equal force to the young lieutenant from civil life.

Immediately after the examination is concluded each candidate should inform the adjutant general of the army where mail matter will reach him, so that he may receive an early notification as to the result of his examination.

The successful candidates receive appointments as second lieutenants in the army, and receive pay as such from date of acceptance, but, as before remarked, all traveling and other expenses must be borne by the candidate until he has joined his first station. He is allowed thirty days' delay in reporting for duty, to enable him to procure proper uniform, equipments, etc. Uniforms may be obtained from military tailors in New York city, Lancaster, Pa., Washington, Philadelphia, and other cities. The best uniforms are always the cheapest in the long run; but a lieutenant, on first joining, will do well to provide himself with a fatigue coat and trousers made from a little cheaper grade of material for rough service, in addition to a fatigue suit of the best quality. Dress coats should always be made by first-class tailors, and from the best of material. Equipments may be purchased from firms in the large cities, and it is never good policy for an officer to purchase anything in this line except it is of superior quality.

Every officer should provide himself with one full-dress uniform, one undress uniform, an overcoat, helmet, shoulder knots, sword and sword knot, dress belt, undress belt, forage cap, and a dozen pairs of white lisle thread gloves. A cape, though not a necessity, is one of the most useful articles in an officer's outfit. The entire cost of these articles, exclusive of the cape, is about two hundred and fifty dollars.

EXAMINATION (CIVIL APPOINTMENTS).

Arithmetic.

1. Multiply $7/15 \times 8/18 \times 15/42 \times 26/50$. Answer in lowest terms.

2. Divide thirty-two and twenty-six thousandths by fifty-seven ten thousandths.

3. Extract the square root of 73·344231.

4. Extract the cube root of 54·010152.

5. If $3/7$ of an article is sold for what $3/5$ of it cost, what is the gain per cent?

6. A workman now earning $2.42 per day has had his wages twice increased 10 per cent: what did he get before the increase?

7. A square lot contains $2\frac{1}{2}$ acres: what is the length of the side in feet?

8. The diameter of a circle is 65 centimetres: what is the area in square inches?

9. How much will it cost to carpet a parlor 18 feet square with carpeting $\frac{3}{4}$ of a yard wide at $1.50 per yard?

10. A note for $470.66 drawn at 60 days is discounted at a bank at 6 per cent: what are the proceeds?

11. In one year and four months $311.50 amounted to $336.42 at simple interest. Find rate per cent.

12. A cubical measure contains $1\frac{1}{2}$ litres. What is the length of an edge in centimetres?

Algebra.

1. Simplify $3a - \{a + b - [a + b + c - (a + b + c + d)]\}$.

2. Multiply $a^{2m} - a^m y^m + y^{2m}$ by $a^m + y^m$.

3. Divide $\frac{2}{3}b^3 + \frac{11}{8}bd^2 - \frac{443}{270}b^2 d - \frac{5}{12}d^3$ by $\frac{3}{2}b - \frac{5}{3}d$.

4. Resolve into factors $3x^4 - 6x^3 + 9x^2$.

5. Find H. C. F. of $x^3 - 1$, $x^3 - 2x^2 - 1$, $x^3 - 2x + 1$.

6. Find the L. C. M. of $6x^3 - 11x^2 y + 2y^3$ and $9x^3 - 22xy^2 - 8y^3$.

FROM CIVIL LIFE. 125

7. Find the quotient of $\dfrac{x^5 - 32}{x - 2}$ by inspection.

8. Solve the equation $(x - 3)(x + 1) = x^2 - 3x + 1$.

9. Three men, A, B, C, pay $1,000 taxes. B pays four times as much as A, and C pays as much as A and B together. How much does each pay?

10. A vessel containing 100 gallons was emptied in 10 minutes by two pipes running one at a time. The first pipe discharged 14 gallons a minute, and the second 9 gallons a minute. How many minutes did each pipe run?

11. Simplify $\dfrac{3}{a+1} - \dfrac{2a-1}{\dfrac{a}{2} - \dfrac{1}{2}}$.

12. Solve the equation $\dfrac{x - b}{c} - \dfrac{bx - c}{a} = abc$.

Geometry.

1. Show how to construct a third proportional to two given lines.

2. State what the area of a trapezoid is equal to, and prove it.

3. In order that a triangle may be constructed, how many parts must be known? Construct the

triangle in the case where two solutions are possible, explaining the limiting cases.

4. The length of the chord of a circular arc is 12 feet, and the height of the arc above the chord is 4 feet: what is the diameter of the circle?

5. From an exterior point a tangent and a secant are drawn to a circle: prove that the tangent is a mean proportional between the whole secant and the part without the circle.

6. Prove that the areas of similar triangles are to each other as the squares on their homologous sides.

7. Upon a given straight line show how to construct a segment of a circle which shall contain a given angle.

8. Find by geometric construction the radius of the circle whose area is equivalent to the sum of the areas of two circles whose radii are 3 and 4 inches respectively.

Trigonometry and Logarithms.

1. (*a*) Explain the reason of the rule for finding the characteristic (or integral part) of the logarithm of a number.

(*b*) Show that (according to this rule) the mantissa (or fractional part) is always *positive*.

(*c*) In what cases is the logarithm, as a whole, positive, and in what cases negative?

2. Compute the value of $\sqrt[5]{\dfrac{(0\cdot012)^3 \times 0\cdot27}{(64)^2 \times 0\cdot00651}}$ by logarithms.

3. Find the functions of 127° 10′ from your trigonometric tables.

4. Two sides of a triangle are 243 feet and 188 feet, and the angle opposite the second side is 42° 20′. Solve the triangle completely.

5. Deduce formulas for sine, cosine, tangent, and cotangent of $2a$ in terms of functions of a.

6. Prove that in any triangle $a^2 = b^2 + c^2 - 2bc \cos A$.

7. Given $\cos A = \sin (45° - \frac{1}{2} A)$. Find A.

8. For what values of x is the expression $\sin x + \cos x$ positive, and for what values negative? Represent the result by a drawing in which the sectors corresponding to the negative values are shaded.

9. Two sides and included angle of a triangle are 2,416, 1,712, and 30°; and two sides and included angle of another triangle are 1,948, 2,848, and 150°. Find the sum of their areas.

10. A tower is situated on the bank of a river. From the opposite bank the angle of elevation of the tower is 60° 13′, and from a point 40 feet more

distant the elevation is 50° 19'. Find the breadth of the river.

Elements of Surveying.

1. What is surveying?

2. Explain the different chains used in measuring lines, giving their lengths, uses, etc.

3. Show how to measure a line, the end of which is invisible from the beginning and intermediate points.

4. State the use of verniers, and give the general rule for reading a vernier.

5. What are the general uses of the transit or theodolite, and explain the method of measuring a horizontal angle with the transit or theodolite.

6. Show how to determine the latitude and departure corresponding to any distance and bearing.

7. Suppose the length and bearing of a side of a field are missing from the field notes: how could you find them by use of the remaining field notes?

8. What do you understand by magnetic declination or variation of the needle? What is an agonic line?

9. Show how the public lands north of the Ohio and west of the Mississippi Rivers are laid out into townships and sections, giving area of each.

10. Give a general description of the plane table and surveyors' level and the principal uses of each.

Grammar.

(Time allotted: three hours.)

1. Define grammar.

2. Name and define the parts of speech, and give an example of each.

3. What is gender? Give the feminine form of youth, emperor, czar, peer, viscount, tutor, and friar.

4. Give plural of beef, radius, staff, valley, deer, apparatus, court-martial, and mouthful.

5. What is comparison of adjectives? Compare many, ill, much, front, and eastern.

6. Parse the words in the following sentence: Terrestrial happiness is of short continuance; the brightness of the flame is wasting its fuel; the fragrant flower is passing away its odors.

7. Correct the following sentences, and give the reason for each correction:

He will maintain his cause though he loses his estate.

If I was to write he would not regard it.

The work has been finished last week.

We hoped to have seen you.

The account of these transactions were incorrect.
Which of all these patterns is the prettier?
The house is situated pleasantly.
Every person is accountable for their own conduct.

8. Dictation: Write and punctuate the following:

The impenitent sinner whom mercy empowers,
Dishonors that goodness which seeks to restore;
As the sands of the desert are watered by showers,
Yet barren and fruitless remain as before.

Spelling.

Apostrophe.	Garrulous.
Battalion.	Hygiene.
Penance.	Indigenous.
Diligence.	Isosceles.
Separate.	Javelin.
Mucous.	Metonymy.
Abstemious.	Naphtha.
Aëronaut.	Omniscient.
Connoisseur.	Referable.
Exhilarate.	Unctuous.

Geography.

(Time allotted: three hours.)

1. How are latitude and longitude reckoned? How does a degree of latitude in latitude 20° compare with a degree in latitude 80°?

2. Define climate, and name three causes affecting climate.

3. How is the land and water in the Eastern and Western hemispheres distributed?

4. Locate Penobscot Bay, Gulf of Bothnia.

5. Name three Asiatic rivers emptying into the Arctic Ocean.

6. Bound France, and describe the courses of three rivers of that country.

7. Locate Odessa, Sheffield, Vera Cruz, Marseilles, Copenhagen, Belfast, Barcelona, Hamburg, St. Petersburg.

8. Name the European states having possessions in Asia.

9. Through what waters would a vessel sail in going from London to Canton?

10. Name the political divisions and governments of North America.

11. Name the States and Territories of the United States.

12. Bound and locate the capitals of Ohio, Georgia, South Dakota, Oregon, Massachusetts.

13. Name the waters in their order through which a vessel would sail in going from Milwaukee to Kansas City.

14. Locate the following: Wheeling, Duluth, Lowell, Louisville, Bangor, Toledo, Santa Fé, San Diego, Seattle, Des Moines.

15. Describe what is meant by standard time.

History.

(Time allotted: three hours.)

1. What were the early discoveries and explorations made by England, France, and Spain?

2. When and by what nations were the following States settled: Virginia, Georgia, Maryland, Massachusetts, New York?

3. Name the colonial wars in their order, and state cause and result of each.

4. Name the original thirteen colonies in their order, and give form of government of each at Revolutionary War.

5. Why was the battle of Saratoga important?

6. Name six battles of the Revolution—three in the North and three in the South.

7. When was the present form of government inaugurated?

8. Where was the principal theatre of the land operations of the War of 1812?

9. How do the land and naval operations compare in importance?

10. When and where was the last battle of this war fought?

11. What Presidents died in office? By whom succeeded in each case?

12. What territory has been acquired since the Revolution?

13. Give the causes and the result of the Mexican War.

14. Where was the theatre of operations of this war? Who were the principal generals in command of United States troops?

15. Explain the Electoral Commission, Dred Scott decision, Missouri Compromise, the Trent affair.

16. What battle terminated the invasion of Pennsylvania in 1863?

17. Give the names of the commanders of the opposing forces, and state which army was victorious, in the following battles: Vicksburg, Chicamauga, Nashville, Port Hudson, Missionary Ridge,

Chancellorsville, Malvern Hill, Knoxville, and Antietam.

18. In what States did slavery exist? How was it abolished?

19. Name an important event in connection with Anthony Wayne, Eli Whitney, Henry Clay, Roger Williams, George H. Thomas, Alexander Hamilton, George Bancroft, O. H. Perry.

20. What is meant by the English revolution of 1688?

21. What is the difference between the English Constitution and ours?

22. What changes have taken place in the French Government since 1789?

23. What important territorial changes have taken place in the Italian peninsula since 1850?

24. Name four important European wars since 1850, and where was the theatre of war in each case?

25. Give the important political questions now (1891) receiving attention in the following countries: Great Britain, Brazil, Italy, Chili, Russia.

Name the books you have studied on history.

Constitutional and International Law.

(Time allotted: three hours.)

1. What were the Articles of Confederation? By what were they replaced?

2. What are the co-ordinate branches of the Federal Government? Name one subject over which each has exclusive control.

3. What is the legislative power, and in whom vested?

4. Describe the veto power.

5. Over what subjects do the States retain jurisdiction?

6. Over what subjects does the Federal Government have exclusive jurisdiction?

7. How may the Constitution be amended?

8. How are new States admitted into the Union?

9. In whom is the appointing power vested by Congress?

10. By what department of Government is the validity of law determined?

11. What is an unconstitutional law?

12. To what do the thirteenth, fourteenth, and fifteenth amendments refer?

13. What is a city of the United States according to the Constitution?

14. How is the President elected, and how succeeded in case of death or other disability?

15. How are Senators and Representatives chosen, and what does each class represent?

16. Over what portion of territory does the United States exercise exclusive control?

17. What is impeachment? Who may be impeached? Who impeaches, and who tries an impeachment?

18. What are territories, and by whom created?

19. What are the provisions of law on the subject of quartering troops?

20. Can the Government create religious establishments?

21. What is international law—public and private?

22. What is the territory of a State?

23. What are the high seas? Over what portions do States exercise control?

24. What is meant by naturalization?

25. How is the national character of an individual determined?

26. What are consuls, and what are their duties?

27. Give some methods less severe than war by which international disputes may be adjusted?

28. Define neutrality.

29. What is contraband of war?

30. What is extradition?

What books on constitutional and international law have you studied?

APPENDIX.

APPENDIX.

COURSE OF STUDY AND BOOKS USED AT THE MILITARY ACADEMY.

(Books marked thus * are for reference.)

First Year—Fourth Class.

MATHEMATICS:
Davies's Elements of Algebra.
Davies's Legendre's Geometry.
Ludlow's Elements of Trigonometry.
Davies's Surveying.
Church's Analytical Geometry.

MODERN LANGUAGES:
Keetels's Analytical and Practical French Grammar.
Keetels's Analytical French Reader.
* Spiers and Surenne's Dictionary.
Whitney's Essentials of English Grammar.

Hart's Manual of Rhetoric and Composition.
Abbott and Seeley's English Lessons for English People.
Abbott's How to Write Clearly.
* Webster's Dictionary.

HISTORY, GEOGRAPHY, AND ETHICS:
Lectures in Ethics, and in Universal History.

DRILL REGULATIONS OF ARTILLERY AND INFANTRY:
Practical Instruction in the Schools of the Soldier, Company, and Battalion.
* Blunt's Firing Regulations for Small Arms.
Practical Instruction in Artillery.

USE OF THE SWORD, ETC.:
Instruction in Fencing and Bayonet Exercise, and Military Gymnastics.

SECOND YEAR—THIRD CLASS.

MATHEMATICS:
Church's Analytical Geometry.
Church's Descriptive Geometry, with its Application to Spherical Projections.
Bass's Introduction to the Differential Calculus.
Church's Calculus.
Church's Shades, Shadows, and Perspective.

APPENDIX. 143

Johnson's Treatise on the Method of Least Squares.

MODERN LANGUAGES:

Keetels's Analytical and Practical French Grammar.

Borel's Grammaire Française.

Bôcher's College Series of French Plays.

Roemer's Cours de Lecture et de Traduction. Vols. I and II.

* Spiers and Surenne's Dictionary.

DRAWING:

Topography and plotting of Surveys with lead pencil, pen and ink, and colors; construction of the various problems in Descriptive Geometry, Shades and Shadows, and Linear perspective and Isometric projections; practical surveying in the field.

* Reed's Topographical Drawing and Sketching, including Photography applied to Surveying.

DRILL REGULATIONS OF ARTILLERY, INFANTRY, AND CAVALRY:

Practical Instruction in the Schools of the Soldier, Company, and Battalion.

Practical Instruction in Small Arms Target Practice.

*Blunt's Firing Regulations for Small Arms.
Practical Instruction in Artillery and Cavalry.

Third Year—Second Class.

Natural and Experimental Philosophy:
Michie's Mechanics, third edition.
Michie and Harlow's Practical Astronomy.
Young's General Astronomy.
Michie's Elements of Wave Motion relating to Sound and Light.

Chemistry, Mineralogy, and Geology:
Bloxam's Chemistry, seventh edition.
Tillman's Elementary Lessons in Heat (revised edition).
Tillman's Essential Principles of Chemistry.
Brown's Eclectic Physiology.
Thompson's Elementary Lessons in Electricity and Magnetism.
Dana's Manual of Mineralogy and Petrography, fifth edition.
Le Conte's Elements of Geology.

Drawing:
Free-hand Drawing and Landscape in black and white.

APPENDIX. 145

Constructive and Architectural Drawing in ink and colors.

* Reed's Topographical Drawing and Sketching, including Photography applied to Surveying.

DRILL REGULATIONS OF ARTILLERY, INFANTRY, AND CAVALRY:

United States Army Artillery Tactics.

Tidball's Manual of Heavy Artillery Service, U. S. A.

United States Army Cavalry Tactics.

Upton's United States Army Infantry Tactics.

Practical Instruction in the Schools of the Soldier, Company, and Battalion.

Practical Instruction in Artillery and Cavalry.

PRACTICAL MILITARY ENGINEERING:

Practical Instruction in the Construction of Pontoon Bridges; in laying Gun Platforms; and in the preparation and application of Siege Materials.

Practical and Theoretical Instruction in Military Signaling.

Fourth Year—First Class.

Civil and Military Engineering, and Science of War:
  Wheeler's Civil Engineering.
  Wheeler's Field Fortifications.
  Mercur's Mahan's Permanent Fortifications, edition of 1887.
  Wheeler's Military Engineering (Siege Operations and Military Mining).
  Mercur's Elements of the Art of War.
  Mahan's Stereotomy.
  * Royal Engineers, Aide-Mémoire, Parts I and II.

Modern Languages:
  Knapp's Spanish Grammar.
  Knapp's Spanish Readings.
  * Seoane's Neuman and Baretti's Dictionary.

Law:
  Davis's International Law.
  Cooley's General Principles of Constitutional Law in the United States.
  Winthrop's Abridgment of Military Law.
  General Orders, No. 100, A. G. O., 1863.

APPENDIX. 147

HISTORY, GEOGRAPHY, AND ETHICS:
Swinton's Outlines of the World's History.
* Labberton's New Historical Atlas and General History.

PRACTICAL MILITARY ENGINEERING:
Practical Instruction in the construction of Pontoon, Trestle, and Spar Bridges; in the preparation and application of Siege Materials; and in laying out Field and Siege works.
Practical Instruction in Military Mining.
Practical Instruction in Military Reconnaissances; in Field Telegraphy, Night Signaling, and the use of the Heliograph.
* Ernst's Manual of Practical Military Engineering.

NATURAL AND EXPERIMENTAL PHILOSOPHY:
Practical Instruction in Astronomy.

DRILL REGULATIONS OF ARTILLERY, INFANTRY, AND CAVALRY:
Practical Instruction in the Schools of the Soldier, Company, and Battalion.
Practical Instruction in Artillery and Cavalry.

ORDNANCE AND GUNNERY:
Metcalfe's Ordnance and Gunnery.
Practical Ballistics.

FORM OF CONDITIONAL APPOINTMENT TO THE MILITARY ACADEMY.

WAR DEPARTMENT,
Washington, ..., 189 .

SIR: You are hereby informed that the President has *conditionally* selected you for appointment as a cadet of the United States Military Academy at West Point, New York.

Should you desire the appointment, you will present yourself for examination before a board of officers at ...., on the .... day of ...., 189 . If it be found that you possess the qualifications required by law and set forth in circular herewith, you will be admitted to the Academy upon reporting in person to the superintendent at West Point on the .... day of ...., 189 .

Should you be found disqualified for military service at an annual physical examination, deficient in studies at the semiannual or annual examinations, or should your conduct reports be unfavorable, you will be discharged from the military service, unless otherwise recommended for special reasons by either the medical or the academic board, but will receive an allowance for traveling expenses to your home.

Your attention is particularly directed to the accompanying circular, and it is to be distinctly understood that this notification confers upon you no right to enter the Military Academy unless your qualifications agree fully with its requirements, and unless you report for examination at the time and place above specified.

You are requested to immediately inform the department of your acceptance or declination of the contemplated appointment upon the above conditions.

Very respectfully,

....

Secretary of War.

....

....

....

NOTE.—No cadet who is reported as deficient, in either conduct or studies, and recommended to be discharged from the academy (military), shall, unless upon recommendation of the Academic Board, be returned or reappointed, or appointed to any place in the army before his class shall have left the academy and received their commissions. (Sec. 1325, Revised Stat. U. S.)

Any cadet dismissed for hazing shall not be eligible to reappointment. (Act of Congress approved March 31, 1884.)

ARTICLES OF AGREEMENT AND OATH OF CADET, UNITED STATES MILITARY ACADEMY.

Each candidate who shall have passed in a satisfactory manner the examination by the board, shall, as soon thereafter as practicable, with the consent of his parent or guardian, if he be a minor and if any he have, sign an engagement for service in the following form in the presence of the superintendent, or of some officer deputed by him:

I, ..., of the State [or Territory] of ...., aged .... years, ... months, do hereby engage (with the consent of my parent or guardian) that, from the date of my admission as a cadet of the United States Military Academy, I will serve in the army of the United States for eight years, unless sooner discharged by competent authority.

....
In the presence of

....

And the cadet shall then take and subscribe an oath or affirmation in the following form:

I, ..., do solemnly swear that I will support the Constitution of the United States, and bear true allegiance to the National Government;

APPENDIX. 151

that I will maintain and defend the sovereignty of the United States, paramount to any and all allegiance, sovereignty, or fealty I may owe to any State or country whatsoever; and that I will at all times obey the legal orders of my superior officers, and the rules and articles governing the armies of the United States.

....
Sworn and subscribed, at ...., this ...... day of ...., eighteen hundred and ...., before me
....

Upon having fully conformed in all respects to the requirements set forth in the preceding paragraph of this article, the candidate shall be admitted as a cadet of the United States Military Academy, and shall receive his warrant as soon as practicable.

FORM OF OATH AND ENLISTMENT PAPER OF A MAN JOINING THE REGULAR ARMY.

THE UNITED STATES OF AMERICA.

STATE OF................. }
City or Town of .... } *ss.:*

I, ..., born in ...., in the State of ...., aged .... years and

.... months, and by occupation a ....,
do hereby acknowledge to have voluntarily .. enlisted,
this .... day of ...., 189 , as a *soldier* in the ARMY OF THE UNITED STATES OF AMERICA, for the period of *five years*, unless sooner discharged by proper authority; and do also agree to accept from the United States such bounty, pay, rations, and clothing as are or may be established by law. And I do solemnly swear (or affirm) that I will bear true faith and allegiance to the UNITED STATES OF AMERICA, and that I will serve them honestly and faithfully against all their enemies whomsoever; and that I will obey the orders of the President of the United States, and the orders of the officers appointed over me, according to the Rules and Articles of War.

.... :SEAL.:

Subscribed and duly sworn to before me this ......
day of ...., A. D. 189 .

....

....

Recruiting Officer.

I certify that I have carefully examined the above-named man agreeably to the General Regu-

APPENDIX. 153

lations of the Army, and that, in my opinion, he is free from all bodily defects and mental infirmity which would, in any way, disqualify him from performing the duties of a soldier.

....
....
Examining Officer.

I certify that I have minutely inspected the above-named man, ..., previous to his ..enlistment, and that he was entirely sober when enlisted; that, to the best of my judgment and belief, he is of lawful age; and that I have accepted and enlisted him into the service of the United States under this contract of enlistment as duly qualified to perform the duties of an ablebodied soldier, and, in doing so, have strictly observed the regulations which govern the Recruiting Service. This soldier has .... *eyes*, ... *hair*, ... *complexion*, is ...... *feet* .... *inches* high.

.... : SEAL. :

....
Recruiting Officer.

FORM FOR THE PHYSICAL EXAMINATION OF A RECRUIT.

Name, ...; age, ...; occupation, ...; birthplace, ...; residence, ...; height,* ....; weight,* ....; chest measurement—expiration, ...; inspiration, ...; nationality of father, ...; of mother, ...

Have you applied for enlistment at any other rendezvous; and, if so, where? ....

What sickness have you had, and at what age? ....

If either parent has died, state cause.............. ....

If brother or sister has died, state cause........... ....

Have you given up any occupation on account of your health or habits? ....

Are you subject to dizziness? ....; to severe headache? ......; to pain in the breast? ......; to fluttering of the heart? ......; to shortness of breath? ......; to colds in the head? ......;

---

* Note height and weight stripped, unless rejected for some absolute disqualification in preliminary examination.

APPENDIX. 155

to coughs? ....; to diarrhœa? ....; to piles? ......; to rheumatism? ......

Do you believe you are sound and well now? ....

Have you had sore eyes? ......

Have you had running from either ear? ......

Have you had fits? If so, how frequently? ....
....

Do you have any difficulty in making or holding your water? ......

Have you had stricture? ......

Have you had gonorrhœa, and when? ....

Have you had a sore of any kind upon your penis, and when? ....

Have you had any swelling about or of your testicles? ......

Have you had a boil near the anus (fistula)? ......

Have you been ruptured? ......

Do you drink intoxicating liquors? If so, to what extent? ....

Have you had the "horrors," and when? ....
....

Have you been hurt upon the head? Answer fully ....

Have you had a sprain? ....; a stiff joint? ......; a bone or joint out of place? ....; a bone broken? ......

Are you subject to sore feet? ......

Mention carefully any other injuries or any surgical operation you may have had in any part of your body, especially burns, cuts, severe bruises, etc.

....

*Have you any one dependent upon you for support? ....

Have you ever been convicted of a felony, or been imprisoned in a jail or penitentiary? ......

NOTE.—The foregoing questions are asked by the surgeon before the applicant is stripped for examination.

†..........................

Applicant.

GENERAL RECRUITING OFFICES, UNITED STATES ARMY.

Albany, N. Y., 513 Broadway.
Baltimore, Md., 303 South Sharp Street.
Boston, Mass. (M. S.), 75 Beach Street.
Boston, Mass. (G. S.), 30 Portland Street.
Bridgeport, Conn., temporary branch.

---

* If answered in the affirmative, recruiting officer before accepting applicant should endeavor to satisfy himself that there is no probability of application being made for the man's discharge on this account.

† Applicant will sign here to the correctness of above statements.

APPENDIX. 157

Brooklyn, N. Y., branch, 61 Fulton Street.
Buffalo, N. Y., 94 Niagara Street.
Camden, N. J., 310 Market Street.
Chicago, Ill. (M. S.), 10 South Clark Street.
Chicago, Ill. (G. S.), 82 West Madison Street.
Cincinnati, Ohio, 166 Plum Street.
Cleveland, Ohio, 142 Ontario Street.
Concord, N. H.
Davenport, Iowa, 124 West Third Street.
Davids Island, New York harbor.
Detroit, Mich., 110 Woodward Avenue.
Evansville, Ind., First and Locust Streets.
Fort Wayne, Ind., Bass Block, Calhoun Street.
Greensborough, N. C., 115 West Market Street.
Harrisburg, Pa., 443 Market Street.
Indianapolis, Ind., 82½ East Washington Street.
Jefferson Barracks, near Columbus, O.
Jefferson Barracks, near St. Louis, Mo.
Knoxville, Tenn., 140 Prince Street.
Louisville, Ky., 504 West Jefferson Street.
Milwaukee, Wis., 445 East Water Street.
Minneapolis, Minn., 119 Nicollet Avenue.
Newark, N. J., 275 Market Street.
New Haven, Conn., 153 Church Street.
New York City (M. S.), 11 Abingdon Square.
New York City (G. S.), 146 Park Row.

Philadelphia, Pa. (M. S.), 939 Spring Garden Street.
Philadelphia, Pa. (G. S.), 1316 Filbert Street.
Pittsburg, Pa., 915 Penn Avenue.
Providence, R. I., 24 North Main Street.
Rochester, N. Y.; 200 East Main Street.
San Francisco, Cal., 1504 Market Street.
Springfield, Mass., 231 Main Street.
St. Louis, Mo., 1126 Pine Street.
St. Paul, Minn., 34 East Seventh Street.
Terre Haute, Ind., 672 Wabash Avenue.
Washington, D. C., 419 Tenth Street, N. W.
Waterbury, Conn., temporary branch.
Wheeling, W. Va., 1131 Main Street.
Wilkesbarre, Pa., Laning Building Public.

FORM OF OATH TAKEN BY ALL COMMISSIONED OFFICERS.

OATH OF OFFICE.

One to accompany the acceptance of every commissioned officer appointed or commissioned by the President in the Army of the United States.

I, ..., having been appointed a .... in the military service of the United States, do solemnly swear (or affirm) that I will support and defend the Constitution of the

APPENDIX.

United States against all enemies, foreign and domestic; that I will bear true faith and allegiance to the same; that I take this obligation freely, without any mental reservation or purpose of evasion; and that I will well and faithfully discharge the duties of the office on which I am about to enter: *So help me God.*

....
....

Sworn to and subscribed before me, at ....
.........., this .... day of ....,
189 .

....
....

TABLE OF PAY ALLOWED BY LAW TO OFFICERS OF THE ARMY.

GRADE.	PAY OF GRADE.		PAY OF OFFICERS IN ACTIVE SERVICE.			MAXIMUM.
	Yearly.	Monthly.	After 5 years' service. 10 per cent.	MONTHLY PAY. After 10 years' service. 20 per cent.	After 15 years' service. 30 per cent.	After 20 years' service. 40 per cent.
Major General.........	$7,500 00	$625 00	......	......	......	......
Brigadier General.....	5,500 00	458 33	......	......	......	......
Colonel...............	3,500 00	291 67	$320 83	$350 00	$375 00	$375 00
Lieutenant Colonel....	3,000 00	250 00	275 00	300 00	325 00	333 33
Major................	2,500 00	208 33	229 17	250 00	270 83	291 67
Captain, mounted.....	2,000 00	166 67	183 33	200 00	216 67	233 33
Captain, not mounted.	1,800 00	150 00	165 00	180 00	195 00	210 00
Regimental adjutant...	1,800 00	150 00	165 00	180 00	195 00	210 00
Regimental quartermaster.	1,800 00	150 00	165 00	180 00	195 00	210 00
First Lieutenant, mounted...	1,600 00	133 33	146 67	160 00	173 33	186 67
First Lieutenant, not mounted...	1,500 00	125 00	137 50	150 00	162 50	175 00
Second Lieutenant, mounted....	1,500 00	125 00	137 50	150 00	162 50	175 00
Second Lieutenant, not mounted.	1,400 00	116 67	128 33	140 00	151 67	163 33
Chaplain..............	1,500 00	125 00	137 50	150 00	162 50	175 00

GREAT COMMANDERS SERIES.
Each, 12mo, cloth, gilt top, $1.50.

Brief biographies of the highest order of excellence, of distinguished American military and naval men, from Washington to Grant. Edited by Gen. JAMES GRANT WILSON.

General Sherman.
By General MANNING F. FORCE.

Admiral Farragut.
By Captain A. T. MAHAN, U. S. N.

General Taylor.
By General O. O. HOWARD, U. S. A.

General Jackson.
By JAMES PARTON.

General Greene.
By Captain FRANCIS V. GREENE, U. S. A.

General J. E. Johnston.
By ROBERT M. HUGHES.

General Thomas.
By HENRY COPPÉE, LL. D.

General Scott.
By General MARCUS J. WRIGHT.

General Washington.
By General BRADLEY T. JOHNSON.

General Lee.
By General FITZHUGH LEE.

General Hancock.
By General FRANCIS A. WALKER.

General Sheridan.
By General HENRY E. DAVIES.

General Grant.
By General JAMES GRANT WILSON.

D. APPLETON AND COMPANY, NEW YORK.

A PICTORIAL HISTORY OF THE WAR WITH SPAIN.

Cannon and Camera.

Sea and Land Battles of the Spanish-American War in Cuba, Camp Life, and the Return of the Soldiers. Described and illustrated by J. C. HEMMENT. With over one hundred full-page pictures taken by the Author, and an Index. Large 12mo. Cloth, $2.00.

"Accurate as well as picturesque. . . . Mr. Hemment las done his work well. In point of faithful realism there has thus far been nothing better in the whole war literature."—*Boston Journal.*

"Clever and picturesque. . . . Over one hundred capital instantaneous photographs illustrate Mr. Hemment's well-written record, and not the least of the book's recommendations is the outspoken simplicity of its style, and the strong impression it makes upon the reader of being the uninfluenced evidence of an eyewitness who 'draws the thing as he sees it' and without exaggeration or prejudice."—*Sunday School Times.*

Recollections of the Civil War.

By CHARLES A. DANA. With Portrait. Large 12mo. Cloth, gilt top, uncut, $2.00.

"The book will rank among the trustworthy sources of knowledge of the civil war."—*New York Evening Post.*

"Mr. Dana's official position as Assistant Secretary of War while the rebellion was in progress gave him exceptional opportunities of observation which he was keen to take advantage of, while his rare gift of terse and vivid expression enabled him to record what he saw in a series of pen pictures that are little less than instantaneous photographs. The feature *par excellence* of these reminiscences is their interesting character. . . . He tells you briefly but graphically what he saw, heard, or did himself. One gains a very real and personal knowledge of the war from these recollections."—*Chicago Times-Herald.*

D. APPLETON AND COMPANY, NEW YORK.

MILITARY TEXT-BOOKS.

Points in Minor Tactics.

Compiled and arranged in an elementary manner for the Infantry of the National Guard of the United States. By Captain CHARLES A. SMYLIE, Twelfth Infantry, N. G. N. Y. With Illustrations. 12mo. Cloth, $1.00. (Second edition just issued.)

Major-General WESLEY MERRITT, U. S. A., says of the second edition of this book, "I regard it as a valuable addition to the 'handbooks' of the Army."

Field-Marshal Lord Roberts, K. P., V. C., commander in chief of the forces in Ireland, writes, "I have read your work with interest, and think it well calculated to fulfill the object with which it was written."

"A work that every member of the National Guard should possess."—*Army and Navy Journal.*

"A book which ought to be placed in the hands of every man in the State troops, and would also make an excellent text book in examinations for promotion."—*New York Evening Sun.*

"A work on minor tactics which is as valuable and applicable to the Canadian militia as to the United States National Guard."—*Canadian Military Gazette.*

Instructions in Military Signaling.

For the Use of the National Guard of the United States. Prepared by Major HOWARD A. GIDDINGS, Brigade Signal Officer, Connecticut National Guard. 16mo. Flexible cloth, 50 cents.

Manual of Arms.

Adapted to the Krag-Jorgensen Magazine Rifle (caliber .30), recently adopted by the United States Army; and also that adapted to the Springfield Rifle (caliber .45), recently adopted by the National Guard. 16mo. Paper, 10 cents.

D. APPLETON AND COMPANY, NEW YORK.

MILITARY TEXT-BOOKS.—(*Continued.*)

Regulations of the Army of the United States,

And General Orders in Force, All Military Law in Force Revised edition, 1895. 8vo. Cloth, $1.50.

Practical Instruction in Minor Tactics and Strategy.

For the Use of the Regular Army and the Militia. By JOHN P. WISSER First Lieutenant, First U. S. Artillery. With Charts and Maps. Approved and authorized as a Text-Book in the U. S. Artillery School. Square 8vo. Cloth, $2 50.

"It is invaluable for the new recruit, and not without value for the man who has drilled and marched, and even commanded for many years."
—*New Haven Journal and Courier.*

Prompt Aid to the Injured.

A Manual of Instruction designed for Military and Civil Use. By ALVAH H. DOTY, M. D., Major and Surgeon, Ninth Regiment, N. G. S. N. Y. With 96 Illustrations. 16mo. Cloth, $1.50.

"A very attractive little work. To the ambulance corps connected with the different military organizations it will be especially valuable, and not less so to all those who may at any time be benefited by the knowledge or application of its excellent precepts and practical suggestions."—*College and Clinical Record.*

D. APPLETON AND COMPANY, NEW YORK.

MILITARY TEXT-BOOKS.

The New Army Drill Regulations.

As approved by the Secretary of War. (Superseding Upton's Tactics, previously the authorized standard for the United States Army.) Illustrated.

For Infantry.
One volume. Bound in leather, with Tuck, 75 cents; in stiff paper covers, 30 cents.

THE SAME, with Appendix, containing Interpretations (replies to inquiries), as published in the *Army and Navy Journal*, by Lieutenant John C. French, Recorder of the Tactical Board. Leather, with Tuck, $1.00; paper, 50 cents.

For Cavalry.
One volume. Leather, with Tuck, $1.00.

For Artillery.
One volume. Leather, with Tuck, $1.00.

For Hospital Corps.
One volume. Leather, 50 cents.

Manual of Guard Duty,
For the United States Army.

As approved by the Secretary of War, January, 1893. Paper, 25 cents; leather, 50 cents.

D. APPLETON AND COMPANY, NEW YORK.

D. APPLETON AND COMPANY'S PUBLICATIONS.

MEMOIRS OF MARSHAL OUDINOT, Duc de Reggio. Compiled from the hitherto unpublished souvenirs of the Duchesse de Reggio by GASTON STIEGLER, and now first translated into English by Alexander Teixeira de Mattos. With two Portraits in Heliogravure. 12mo. Cloth, $2.00.

"The 'Memoirs of Marshal Oudinot' are interesting because they include the history of one of the most brilliant periods the world has ever seen."—*Chicago Evening Post.*

"The reading of this charming, vivacious, and accurate book makes it a continual source of wonder that any one, at this day, should be writing a history of the Napoleonic era. . . . The complete unconsciousness and the exquisite naturalness of the style are charming."—*New York Commercial Advertiser.*

"This frankly loyal and graphic picturing of a great man's true character, seen from the nearest standpoints by a biographer of wonderful keenness, is genuinely refreshing. Vivid and explicit without being unduly sentimental, it is a book distinctly invaluable to and actually inseparable from a study of French history."—*Boston Globe.*

"It is for the side lights of the marshal's life that this book is chiefly valuable, and wonderfully illuminating they are. Besides, there is a never-ending charm in the freshness of the narrative. There is nothing that is dull or monotonous."—*Chicago Journal.*

"Full of new and entertaining material, and has a really significant historical value. . . . These memoirs are noteworthy for their gentleness of tone and their freedom from satire and vituperation. They deal with great events, and their very simplicity and unpretentiousness are evidence of their incontestable merit "—*Boston Beacon.*

"The story of this gallant soldier is of strong romantic interest and makes excellent reading, while the side lights thrown on events of a long period marked by many extraordinary changes are vastly interesting and informing. It is an inspiring and thoroughly delightful volume."—*Providence News.*

"Few French commanders were more popular, both with rulers and with the people. The eventful story of his life, modestly told, is charming in interest."—*Chicago Inter-Ocean.*

"The pages are filled with illustrious names that arouse pleasant or unpleasant memories, and the reader reads eagerly onward, always entertained, frequently enlightened, until the last page is reached. . . . It will be equally welcomed by the student of history and by the general reader." —*Boston Saturday Evening Gazette.*

"Amid the mass of French memorial writing there is none that will be found more attractive, because there is none more genuine than this record."—*Chicago Times-Herald.*

"An extremely interesting addition to historical biography. . . . These memoirs relate the extraordinary career of an extraordinary man. . . . A complete biography, written in an easy, natural, unpretentious style."— *Detroit Free Press.*

D. APPLETON AND COMPANY, NEW YORK.

www.ingramcontent.com/pod-product-compliance
Lightning Source LLC
Chambersburg PA
CBHW031450160426
43195CB00010BB/924